T0123663

OUT OF MY MINDS

CONVERSATIONS WITH MY HIGHER SELF

Maxima Miller

BALBOA.
PRESS

A DIVISION OF HAY HOUSE

Copyright © 2018 Maxima Miller.

All rights reserved. No part of this book may be used or reproduced by any means, graphic, electronic, or mechanical, including photocopying, recording, taping or by any information storage retrieval system without the written permission of the author except in the case of brief quotations embodied in critical articles and reviews.

Balboa Press books may be ordered through booksellers or by contacting:

Balboa Press
A Division of Hay House
1663 Liberty Drive
Bloomington, IN 47403
www.balboapress.com.au
1 (877) 407-4847

Because of the dynamic nature of the Internet, any web addresses or links contained in this book may have changed since publication and may no longer be valid. The views expressed in this work are solely those of the author and do not necessarily reflect the views of the publisher, and the publisher hereby disclaims any responsibility for them.

The author of this book does not dispense medical advice or prescribe the use of any technique as a form of treatment for physical, emotional, or medical problems without the advice of a physician, either directly or indirectly. The intent of the author is only to offer information of a general nature to help you in your quest for emotional and spiritual well-being. In the event you use any of the information in this book for yourself, which is your constitutional right, the author and the publisher assume no responsibility for your actions.

Any people depicted in stock imagery provided by Dreamstime.com are models, and such images are being used for illustrative purposes only. Certain stock imagery © Dreamstime.com

Print information available on the last page.

ISBN: 978-1-5043-1577-7 (sc)
ISBN: 978-1-5043-1578-4 (e)

Balboa Press rev. date: 11/12/2018

Contents

Acknowledgements

To my dear husband I give my never-ending love. You always love me, support me, and believe in me. I greatly appreciate your input, words of wisdom and love.

My deepest gratitude goes to my two daughters for providing me with valuable feedback on the draft of this book, and more so for simply being my daughters. I love you both to the moon and back.

To my editor Wayne H. Purdin, I thank you for your contribution and support. Your suggestions have improved the quality of this book.

A big thank you also to Alexander Selimov, who was one of the very first people to have read my book and who has given me great pointers not only about the book itself but also on publishing options and some related legal matters.

And, last but not least, my thanks go out to all the wonderful people at Balboa Press, who helped me getting my book published.

This book is dedicated

To my loving husband
To my dearest and beautiful daughters
To my soul sister
and to our next generations

Introduction

***

It must have been at least 10 years ago when I started writing this book. The first sections of this book I had already written when I still lived in The Netherlands, but I completed the book only after I moved to Australia.

I was in desperate need of some help, someone to talk to, but there wasn't anyone except for my daughters. I had no money for a psychologist, I had no friends, and I was living a pretty lonely life.

To help myself, I decided to put my life, my struggles, as well as my hopes and dreams on paper, mainly to try to make sense of it all myself.

I wrote sections of this book over several months and years. I wasn't in any rush; I had no intention of publishing it, and I guess you can say it was more like a journal to me.

Then things changed for the better; I found a very loving and caring boyfriend who didn't just care for me but also took care of me, and who later became my husband. Not long after that, I also found some other people I could relate to: good and reliable people who were trying to do the right thing. At the same time, I also got a good job, I was making enough money to live off, and my health was reasonably okay. In other words, my life was better than ever.

My life has greatly improved over the last few years. I have a great life, a great love, a good job, and I'm working toward being healthy and living a healthy live. There's no reason to complain, no reason to spill my guts out on paper anymore. But I was prompted to write again after two events that happened within a period of about nine months.

The first occasion was the passing away of my mother-in-law. I'd only known her for a very short time and had only met her once, but I had liked her instantly. Her passing away was sad, even for me.

What struck me after the funeral was her granddaughters' pain. They told me that they never really new the real woman their grandmother was. They told me their grandmother didn't like talking about certain events in her life. They felt like they had missed out on getting an understanding of why their grandmother was the person she was, what she was really about. I could see and feel that they loved her very much. They clearly also felt that they had missed a part of the story, a part of their heritage. They wanted to understand where they were coming from.

I understood. I didn't know a lot of things about my grandparents and their parents. I knew very little about the history of my family.

Then and there, I realized that writing down your own history and explanation of why you made certain decisions could well be of interest and even of importance to future generations. But that realization alone wasn't enough to motivate me to continue writing; it wasn't until I had a health scare that I really decided to finish this book.

After becoming dehydrated, I ended up in hospital. I'd had a terrible headache for a few days and then I started vomiting and I couldn't keep any food or drinks in. I was also in quite a bit of pain that was caused by an old shoulder injury. My condition wasn't really serious, and the hospital released me after a few hours.

My doctor recommended that I have an MRI of my head, as she was concerned about my headaches. I went for the MRI but wasn't concerned about it at all. I didn't even bother to follow up with my doctor, as I thought it would be a waste of time and money.

A week later however, I received a letter from my doctor, saying, "We have received the results of your MRI and we would like you to come in for a discussion." Well, that didn't sound too good. Normally, your doctor only contacts you when something is wrong.

I made an appointment for the following day. In the meantime, many frightening thoughts were going through my head: "Did they find a brain tumor? Was there anything else wrong? Was I going to die?"

It made me think. If I were going to die soon, what things would I definitely want to do before that? I definitely wanted to do a few specific things before dying. I wanted to see and hold my grandchild. I wanted to marry my boyfriend. If still possible I also wanted to go on a holiday. Finally, I wanted to finish documenting my life.

When I visited my doctor, she told me that the MRI came back all clear, but that she wanted to talk to me about my headaches. She just wanted to see how I was doing. What a fuss for nothing. Well, not really nothing.

It was the trigger for finishing my book. And then by "accident," I found a website about publishing an eBook. That was the first time I thought about the possibility of publishing my story.

And then there's another reason to publish my story. My life has been very eventful, and, on the way, I've learned a lot of things that may be beneficial for anyone reading this book. So, in that sense, you could say that I hope this book will help some people on their personal journey.

This book is not just a memoir. More so, it may be of value to anyone who is interested in the spiritual, supernatural, and self-development.

When you start reading, you'll realize that, from the first page on, it isn't exactly an ordinary story. You'll read some pretty incredible things, and I wouldn't blame you if you can't believe it.

However, this is my story, my memoir, an overview of the events of my life. For me, it's all true, although I have to admit that there are many things I still can't explain myself.

I've written down what I've experienced. This doesn't make it true or untrue; it's merely a record of my experiences. Some experiences are weird, strange, and out of the ordinary, and it would have been easier for me to just exclude them. But I couldn't. It wouldn't have given you, nor my offspring the full story of my life. It would have only given a part of the picture, and any potential next generations would have missed out on the complete story of my life: the weird along with the not so weird. I also prefer to tell an unbelievable truth rather than a believable lie.

The truth, my truth, and your truth is ever changing. Our truth changes while we learn, while we experience new things, while we read or listen, or see. When expanding our understanding of things, our truth expands at the same time. During the process of writing this book, my truth has certainly changed.

To all of my readers, I'd like to say that I hope this book helps you find your truth, I hope that you can relate to some of my stories, I hope that you find something that will help you in your own life, and I hope it makes you feel that you're not as out of your mind as you might sometimes feel.

With Love,

Maxima

You, Me, And I

***

Fire is raging through my body. What the...? It seems like the clock is standing still, but when I look at it, I can still see the little hand moving with each second. Strange. Certainly, time always goes on; or does it? It seems like everything has stopped except for me. My mind is racing, my body feels hot, but I can see goose bumps on the skin of my arms. What's happening? I feel like I've been sucked into a black hole that's me. I feel a bit scared. What's going on?

Then I hear a voice coming out of nowhere...

Hello, Hello...
What happened?

Did I really hear that?

What happened?

I hear the voice again. Maybe I don't really hear it with my ears. It's like a voice in my head. But it's there. No doubt about it. Am I going crazy? Am I paranoid? Am I schizophrenic?

I hear it again.

What happened?

I look around to see if someone is standing behind the door, playing a trick on me. I stand up to have a look, but no one is there. Again, I hear the voice.

Hello…Tell me what happened.

"Uh? What do you mean? Who's there? Who are you?"

You want to talk to me because something has happened.

"Oops, someone must be there. But I can't see anyone. Am I talking to myself? Am I losing my mind?

"Who are you and who says I want to talk to you? I have no idea what you're talking about."

Really? I just noticed you thinking that you're finally ready to talk about all the things that have happened.

"You noticed me thinking? How can you notice me thinking? And who are you?"

You can call me any name you want. It's not important. What's important is that I'm here for you and ready to listen to you. Am I right that you would finally like to talk?

"Uh, yes, that's right, but…"

Just consider me your best friend. If you don't like it, you can always stop talking to me.

"But who are you, and why can't I see you? I hear your voice but I don't see you. Are you real?"

Oh yes, I'm very real. I'm as real as you are.

"Then, are you invisible?"

No, not really. I'm here.

"You confuse me. I can't see you, but you're not invisible. You say you're here and yes, I can hear your voice. But, I don't understand."

Well, there are many, many things you don't understand or don't know. That doesn't make them any less true. I'm here to help. I'm here for you, always and everywhere, in this here and now and in every here and now, without any exception.

"Now you're scaring me. Are you a stalker?"

No, I'm not. I don't need to stalk. I'm simply here to help you, to listen to you, to comfort you, to just be with you.

If it makes is easier to you, please see me as your invisible friend, although I'm not invisible as such.

I'm here to start a conversation with you, the conversation that you'll record in your book.

"What?! I'm not writing a book, I'm writing down events of my life, my life history. But I have no intention to write a book. What makes you say that I'm writing a book? Who are you? What do you want from me? And, are you saying that you and I can talk although I can't see you?"

I'm not invisible as you'll find out. And you and I are already talking this very moment, so why not talk a little more? Even if you believe that this isn't real, what do you have to lose by "pretending" talking to me? And, by the way, I am real.

"That's really, really weird. You want to talk to me, listen to me? You say you want to help me? I don't understand at all. What makes you think I want your help? What makes you believe I want to talk to you?"

Am I wrong in believing that you would like to talk to someone? Haven't you wished for someone to talk to for a very long time?

"Yeah, that's true, but…"

And, haven't you begged for someone to help you? Give you a hand? Help you making sense of all that has happened in your life?

"Yes, kind of, but how can I talk to someone who isn't there?"

But I'm here. I'm here. Do you hear me? I'm HERE. You hear me, so I am.

"Okay, sure. Uhm, all right then, I'm not sure what this is, I don't understand, but tell me what this is all about. What do you want from me?"

I would like to hear your story and help you make sense of what has happened in your life, but for now, just tell me what's going on right now and we'll take it from there.

"I'm reluctant, even a bit scared. I still don't understand who you are or what you want from me exactly."

It's time for you to open up and talk. More than that, it's time for you to let go of fear of what others may or may not think of you. It's time for you to dare to be totally yourself. Your weird self, as you call it. Even though I don't believe you're weird at all.

"You think *I'm* weird? What about this conversation? Isn't this conversation strange at the very least?"

It's only you calling this conversation weird. Those are not my words. It's natural and normal, and I know that, in the end, you'll actually like this conversation. So, what do you say? Are you willing to put your mistrust and your reluctance aside and, instead, just see what happens when we talk?

"Okay then... this is really, really w... I mean strange, but I'll tell you what's going on." Many, many things have happened in my life. It's been like a constant flow of endless events that I've had to deal with. Now that things have somewhat quieted down, I feel I need someone to talk to. But this is so strange. I'm still not sure who you are..."

Okay, I understand you're still a bit confused, but just talk to me. Why do you feel you need to talk right now? You didn't feel the need to talk earlier.

"Yes, I did in a way, but I felt it wasn't the right time."

How come?

"Let me try to explain with a little story… I'm in the ocean, and although I'm a pretty good swimmer, I'm drowning. I'm sinking to the bottom, but every time I get there, I get new strength and push myself up to reach the surface and take a breath of air. Often I'm just able to take one single breath until the next stormy wave is coming up to engulf me and drag me to the bottom once again.

"Sometimes, people in a boat come very close, and I think they're there to help me get onshore. But then, either the next wave comes and they can't help me because they have to help themselves or, instead of helping me, they laugh and push me down under again.

"And I swim and struggle to get any air in my lunges. Sometimes, I'm not even getting to the surface before the next wave hits me. Other times I can get a few breaths of air before the next thing drags me down.

"Like I said, I'm a pretty good swimmer, but it's a constant struggle to get any air at all and I feel I'm drowning, suffocating. I can't get enough air and I don't get any rest in between. My head feels like it's exploding, my body aches and I'm exhausted from continuously swimming and getting no rest at all.

"The truth is, I don't know how much longer I can go on. At times, I think of giving up. I want to sink to the bottom and simply die. But I don't. No matter how much I want to give up, I'm thinking of those few people in the boat who actually want to help me. I owe it to them to keep on trying, and maybe one day, I can stay on the surface for a bit longer and reach the shore. I don't want to make these people feel sad or guilty because they couldn't save me. I would feel like that would be my fault because I gave up. I don't want to do that to anybody, especially not to the people who really try to get me out of the water.

"So I keep on swimming, struggling, and hoping that maybe one day, I can freely breathe the air around me. Yes, I still have a little hope left and a tiny belief that it will actually happen and that I can get to shore. That, and the knowledge that there are people in a boat trying to help me, is what I'm holding onto.

"At this moment in my life, I have my head out of the water and I'm taking a couple of breaths of air. In the distance, I can see the shore, the end of a hard time. I'm not there yet, but I have hope I'll get there. Now, I can take some time to talk, little by little. Earlier on, I was afraid that talking would be like drowning again, opening my mouth and taking the risk it would fill up with water again. Also, I was afraid that it would be like opening up a tap and spilling out the water in my lungs with no stopping. I couldn't let go, because I was no way near a solution yet. I couldn't rest yet.

"Now that things are going a little bit better, I can take the time to reflect, and try to understand. I would like to talk to someone who may be able to see things from a different point of view, who can help me get the whole picture and bring to me insights that I would have missed on my own. I would like to talk to someone who's open-minded because I realize that many things I'm going to say are pretty unbelievable. Unbelievable, but all true. Well, at least, it's my truth.

"I'd like to talk to someone who's able to think outside the box, who's patient, and who understands that, for me, it's not about what actually happened, but about how I reacted to it and how I still react to it. I would like to talk to someone who can help me find other, better, healthier, and more effective ways to deal with my past."

I believe that I understand what you're saying. Sometimes the only way to get through is to make do, because if you don't, you'll never get there, or it will only stop you or slow you down on your path.

"Yes, exactly."

But why did you choose me to talk to?

"What do you mean? I didn't choose to talk to you. I can't even see you. You started talking to me, remember? I only kind of hear you in my head."

That's true. But you did choose to talk to me. Let me repeat that. You may not consciously realize it, but you did choose to talk to me. You may think this is all a bit strange, but it's not, and you'll get used to it. So again, why did you choose me to talk to?

"I'm not sure..."

Really?

"Really!"

Well, I know you don't want to hear this, but you actually are sure. You do know.

"Oh, but if you know I do know, then why are you asking? That doesn't make much sense to me."

I think it all makes perfectly sense to you. You just don't really want to admit it to yourself because you believe it's all a little strange. However, it isn't as strange as you may think. There are many things in life that are stranger. And this actually is quite simple.

"Hmmm...if what I think is correct, then it's simple, but unlikely."

Yes? So...?

"If I say this out loud, then people may think that I'm schizophrenic. Which, by the way, I'm not.

"How can I explain? I think I chose to talk to you because you truly understand me. It's because maybe you're me. I'm talking to myself I think."

YES! That's correct. But I'm wondering if you really understand. Can you explain to me how you see this?

"To be honest, I don't understand anything of this. Can you please explain?"

You're talking to the whole of yourself. I know you and you know me. I'm that part of you, like the inner you, your soul, your light, that has all the answers,

7

has all the knowledge about you/me. You don't need to find someone else, as your soul and every cell in your body know ALL there is to know, as it's a part of the ALL…

"And you'll help me with your empathy, with your kindness, but also with your structural advice and knowledge and I know that, if needed, you'll tell me the harder truth, even if I don't want to hear it. Talking to you (me) is merely a way to access the relevant information and deeper truths that my conscious mind isn't able to find on its own.

"So you could say that you're the part that knows; I'm the part of me that moves, that takes action. I'm the physical part: the flesh, blood, and bones; you're the spiritual side, the soul, the core. You're my higher self. But we aren't separate; we're ONE."

Correct! Yes, that sums it up pretty nicely.

Question for you: knowing this, aren't you afraid that you'll give yourself only the answers that you want to hear?

"That would probably happen if I would talk to only a part of me. But, I believe I can talk to the complete me, who has all the knowledge, wisdom, and experiences. So what my physical me and my ego don't want to hear or understand, the spiritual part of me does understand for me. My spiritual part will guide my physical expression of myself; at least, I hope so. And, if so, then I assume that my spiritual part is wiser and will, therefore, guide and instruct my physical me, even if my physical part tries to resist."

How do you think you'll do that? Talking to the complete you seems pretty weird to me.

"What? What are you talking about now? First, you start talking to me and make it all sound very natural and normal, and now you're questioning it?

You're confusing me.

"Okay, for some reason I think I can talk to you. I believe you're also sometimes trying to confuse me, simply to test me and to see if I'm really up for a conversation like this one we're having right now. I think I have always believed I can access the knowledge of my whole self."

Oh, are you saying that you're not your whole self right now?

"No, that's not what I'm saying. I'm saying that most of the time, I'm only aware of a part of me. I know that I'm more than what can be seen, I know that I'm more than my body, more than my consciousness and unconsciousness. I have access to my whole me. I believe I talked with the whole me before and I know I can do it again."

Okay, let's say you really can. How are you planning to do that?

"Well, funny you should ask because I already AM talking to me! You of all should know that. But okay, I'll explain. From experience, there are different ways to do that. Automatic writing is one of them. Yes, I know, it sounds weird."

What do you mean by automatic writing?

"Sometimes, I sit in front of my computer and it's like the words come without me having to think about it. It's like my fingers type the right letters without me realizing what I'm writing, but when I read it later, it suddenly makes sense. Automatic writing is the process of channeling my higher self directly into writing. To me, this comes naturally, but anyone can easily learn this. Anyone can search the Internet for "automatic writing" and find information on how to do this.

"And while we're on this topic, I think there are other ways to talk to the whole me as well such as meditation and praying or talking to the universe.

"And before you ask, talking to the universe I do by just thinking of something, saying something, or asking something out loud and/or directing my thoughts to the universe or anyone/anything up there or down here that may be able to help me. Actually, I think it's very much like praying. I believe I receive answers by suddenly hearing words in my ears, by picking up a book at the certain page and randomly picking a sentence or paragraph. At other times, I just seem to know things or have visions that make things clear."

Of course, you mean that you have dreams.

"No. I'm not only dreaming. For me, there's a big difference between a vision and a dream. In dreams, I always seem to have a problem seeing things. It's like my vision is blurred, like when I don't wear my glasses in waking life. When I have a vision, all is crystal clear and I still remember details of the vision years later."

Hmmm, all right, you haven't completely convinced me yet, but I'm willing to go with it. If it works for you, then I guess it'll work for me too.

Let's talk…

Reflection:

- **Everyone is intuitive and can experience this in different ways.**
- **You're more than you can see.**
- **Within you, when you access your higher self, you can find all answers, if you choose to look for them.**

Help, I Need Somebody

***

Where would you like to start?

"To be honest, I don't know. There's so much to talk about. I'm actually afraid that after talking to you, I'll find out that I forgot to talk about certain parts. At the moment, it seems like I have to unpack many, many boxes and I don't know where to start."

Okay, why don't you start by telling me what's bothering you right now?

"Even this isn't something easy. There are so many things going through my mind right now. But I'll try to start with something at least. "Actually, I'd like to talk about what scares me at this moment.

"As I told you, I've been through quite a bit and, although things are a lot better, they're far from perfect. I'm doing a bit better than surviving now, but I'm far from really living. At times, I'm afraid I'll never reach that point when everything or most things are okay and I can live and enjoy my life. I know that that sounds pretty negative, and most of the time, I'm a lot more positive. However, in the back of my mind, I'm afraid of having to struggle for my entire life and never reaching that point when I can lean back, relax, and breathe in fresh, clean air."

It sounds like you find your life a constant battle, a never-ending battle.

"Yes and no. In my negative moments, I do feel like that, yes. But I also realize that all that has happened has had an impact on who I am today. And today, I like myself. I believe I'm a good person. I'm far from perfect, but I'm a good person. Today I know who I am. I'm strong and have an enormous inner power. I'm kind and loving and have this incredible zest for life. Although I have to admit that this zest for life sometimes gets blocked out. But I believe that's the real me, the core of what I truly am. It's like my whole being wants to suck up life like a sponge, the good and the bad. I'm a very passionate person in many ways.

"I give life all I have to give. I put all my energy, all my being in everything I do: work, love, relationships, education, singing, or dancing. I believe I wouldn't be able to do it any differently. I wouldn't want to be anyone different. When I die, I want to know for myself that I've given this life everything I have to give, like I don't want to miss out on anything. I just feel like I often don't have the energy to do so."

Hmm, great that you want to live your life to the full, but what does that have to do with your life being a battle? I don't get it. From what you're saying, I understand that you're happy with yourself and that actually you like your life, because you live it to the fullest. On the other hand, you're more or less admitting that you find your life a constant battle. So tell me, what is it really? Of course, I know the answer, but I want you to discover it for yourself and say it out loud.

"Well, if you know it too, then why don't you help me and tell me because I honestly don't know."

The thing is that you DO know. You just don't like the truth. You don't like admitting it. I could help you out, but it's better that you recognize the answer yourself. I want you to say it for yourself, because that will help you in better understanding what's going on.

"That's kind of mean."

No, that's called tough love. Just try to put it in words and I'll help you from there. You believe it's a bad thing, but it isn't. It just is.

"I thought you were on my side."

I am. I'm you; remember?

"Then why don't you want to help me?"

I challenge you to think for yourself because that's the only way you can grow. The only way to grow, to experience, to feel is in your relative world. The part of you that's me already KNOWS, but the part of me that's you, can actually FEEL, EXPERIENCE, DISCOVER.

"Are you saying here that you can't feel or experience things?"

I'm saying that I know all there is to know, and that through my expression of you being me and me being you, being one, I can feel and experience and know at the same time. That's called being "whole."

"Does that mean that without me you wouldn't be able to – let's call it – experience?"

No, there's no separation between you and me. You and I are one.

So why can't you "experience"?

I do "experience." I do that through the part of me that's you. You're an expression of me; therefore, you're me and I'm you. You're the part that merely feels. I'm the part that knows all there is to know. But we're not separate, although I understand that often feel that way. We're ONE. And you know we're one; otherwise, you wouldn't be talking to me.

"Yes, I do know that. Don't ask me how I know that. I just know even though I can't prove it. That's pretty weird."

I can understand why you say it's weird. Hmmm, you seem to like that word. And there's a lot more stuff that you would qualify as weird, so much so that you wouldn't be able to comprehend even if you were the smartest person on earth. If you tried, your brain would overload.

"Oh, it sounds like I'm pretty stupid."

How on earth can you say that? You're not stupid. You're very smart. You know all there is to know because you and I are one. Once again, you and I

ARE NOT separate. And because I know all there is to know, you can access this "library" of all there is to know. It's just like a real library; you only read the books that you're interested in or that you need. You wouldn't be able to read it all and you don't need to read it all.

For you, as the part of us who experiences, are very smart to understand that another part of you knows. I know you know; otherwise, we wouldn't be talking right now. I also know that you know how to access that "library" that's me. You can always access me, because we're one.

I cannot tell you times enough that we're ONE. There's no separation. Please, don't just know that, but also feel that. I understand that, sometimes, you seem to forget that. But it's not that you've forgotten; it's because you're too lazy to go to the "library" pick a book and read it. You only come to me when you're in desperate need of answers. In that way, you're just stubborn and arrogant.

"Thanks, I really needed to hear that last part."

Yes, you did.

"I'm being sarcastic here."

Okay, so apart from being stubborn and arrogant, you're also sarcastic.

"Great! Instead of helping me, you're putting me down now."

No, I'm not. I'm making a point.

"And the point being…?"

The point is that you could go to the "library" more often. You would feel more – what you call – "in control" and, therefore, more relaxed. The thing is that you know this. You know that I'm right, but, sometimes, you refuse to act upon it.

"Okay, you could be right about that."

Excuse me?

"Yes, yes. You ARE right."

Alright. Let's get back to the question I asked before and that you have so carefully tried to avoid answering.

The question was "How come you find your life a battle while, on the other hand, you're happy with yourself and feel you're living your life to the fullest?"

By the way – I need to mention this – I don't believe you're living your life to the fullest. You're living a pretty full life, but you could do more, be more. And, you know it.

"Yeah, yeah, of course, I know it. We're one, remember?"

I'm glad you're starting to remember too.

"I'm being sarcastic again."

I know. You seem to be getting sarcastic when you hear things you don't really want to hear.

"God, so this is what they call tough love?"

Yes, and you better get used to it. Now, can I finally get an answer to the question I asked?

"Okay. I'm happy with my life because it's never boring and I get to experience a lot of different things that many other people never get to experience in their entire life. I also realize that whatever battle I've fought, whatever I've been through, has contributed to being who I am today. And I told you before that I'm happy about who I am today. So, in that sense, the battles of my life have contributed to feeling happy about myself. Of course, I don't like having to fight all those battles."

That's a really good start. It's not the full answer, though, and you know it. So let me help you by asking the next question.

Who says that you have to fight all those battles and who says that you have to fight all those battles to be happy?

"Uh, no one, actually."

So, why do you fight them?

"Because they occur and I have to do something about them."

Why do they occur?

"I don't know. It just happens."

Really?

"Yes."

NO!

"No?"

NO! You know it doesn't just happen.

"I know? You're saying it doesn't just happen? Are you saying it happens for a reason?"

Yes. And you're going to tell me exactly what the reason is.

"How would I know what the reason is?"

Because you're me!

"I know that you're me and I'm you. But what does that have to do with the reason behind my battles?"

Because through me, you can "look-up" the reason, if you would really want to. Do you really want to know the answer to that what you already know?

"Do you mean that I can go to the "library" to find out, but that I already know the answer?"

Exactly. You already know the answer, but you don't like it. That's why you're trying to avoid it and pretend you don't know. Even while you're typing this, you're taking unnecessary breaks to avoid answering it.

"Bummer. I really don't like saying this and a part of me isn't even sure that this is the answer. But, for some reason, I believe I'm responsible for the battles in my life, like I create them or, at the very least, choose them. And, most likely, I create them because they'll contribute to my life. They've contributed to being happy about who I am, that's for sure. I suppose it all has to do with relativity. Being happy only has real meaning if you know what it is to be unhappy. We only experience heat, because we experience cold and the other way around. Something can't really be experienced if the opposite doesn't exist, such as experiencing the lower end of something makes you able to fully experience the upper end of it.

"Or maybe I'm creating them, because there's something I have to learn. Does that make sense? Also, let's assume that I'm really creating or at least choosing my own battles, then my next question is, How am I doing that and how can I choose differently? And, does that mean that you use me to experience, because you only know? That doesn't feel right. It's like you use me to do the dirty work! That certainly doesn't make me happy. It's unfair. And you, most of all, should know how I feel about unfair situations."

Very good, you finally came up with an honest answer and you even found the reason for it. I'm not letting you do the dirty work. If you believe that, you would also have to admit that I let you do all the great happy work. But you're forgetting that we're one. We're not separate where one has to experience all the pleasures and the other one experiences only pain. I get to experience all that you do, because we're one. The human form in which you experience yourself is an expression of you/me, but as you said yourself, you're much more than you can comprehend in this human form. And let me give you some more shocking news; not only are we one, but we're one with everything else there is. We're an expression of the ALL.

You were asking how you're creating your own battles and, of course, also all your "good" experiences and how you can choose what you experience. There are actually two parts to the answer. First, human beings create events and their experiences by thought, intention, emotion, and action.

"I've heard something very similar before and I think I kind of get the concept, but can you please explain how it works because, although I seem to know, I haven't been able to bring it into practice?"

Actually, you have brought it into practice, every time, again, with everything in your life, and, sometimes, you were even aware of it and thought it was a coincidence or a miracle. In fact, it was all created by you.

"You mean the time when I found out where help would come from?"

Yes, exactly, that's only one of the countless occasions, but a very beautiful, touching, and clear occasion.

"I was deeply touched by the moment. I had just made a new friend two weeks before and was somehow intrigued by his name. For some reason I thought his name had some kind of important meaning. I looked it up on the Internet and was actually disappointed that it meant "Lord of God." It didn't have much meaning to me at that moment. But days later, I was driving back home, coming from work. I was feeling down, as I knew that my work contract would soon end and I didn't have any work lined up after that. I wasn't in a position not to work and didn't want to end up in poverty as I had before. So I was feeling pretty desperate as I was driving home. I remember saying out loud, 'God, I need help. Can you please show me where to get help, right now?' As soon as I had said this, I looked up to the right and saw this large billboard saying: 'Your help comes from the Lord of God.' I remember having tears in my eyes, as I knew instantly that my help would come from my beautiful new friend."

This is a great and touching example. I remember us getting goose bumps.

"My friend turned out to be the one helping me, although not in the way that I expected. He was a taxi driver, and every time I had to work in another city and catch a flight, he would get me to the airport or pick me up. I liked him from the very first time and found that I could talk to him about anything. I told him about my work, that it would end soon and that I was also still waiting for my pay for work that I had finished 3 months ago.

"As a joke, he said to me that I could always become a taxi driver. That way I would always have work in between my contracts and always have money coming in without delay. He actually mentioned that a few times over a couple of weeks, and I started to like the idea. I'd always liked driving and was often complimented on my driving style and great sense of direction. Driving a taxi would help me to make money when I didn't have work.

"Before I knew it, I enrolled myself in a taxi drivers training, and four months after I met my friend, I received my Taxi Authority and was ready to drive my first shift. He also helped me with a uniform and lots of advice and tips and he put me in contact with taxi companies I could drive for. I could always count on him for help and advice.

"I absolutely loved driving. I loved the contact with my passengers and all the different stories they would tell me. I loved giving just that bit of extra service to the elderly by helping them bring their groceries inside. And after just 3 months of driving, I was awarded as Taxi Driver of the Month for providing a great service.

"The driving brought enough money in, but I really had to put in the hours to make that money. Most of the weeks, I would drive 12 hours a day for 7 days. That, combined with being a single mom with three kids at home, completely burned me out and I couldn't drive anymore. Also, I needed to drive so much that I didn't have any time left to put in my IT consulting business and find new work.

"So after 9 months of driving, I found myself burnt out with no work and no money coming in. I kind of crashed. It wasn't a real accident, but it was very close, and I was just overworked. But I'll never forget that beautiful moment when I found out that my new friend would be the one to help me, as he did many, many times. I'm forever grateful for all that he did for me. He is a great soul, and I'll never forget his kindness."

Going back to the moment that you asked and then received help, what do you believe happened at that moment?

"Well, simply, I asked for help and received it."

Do you understand why?

"I'm not sure, but you said earlier that human beings create by thought, intention, emotion, and action. So I think that the thought was there, the intention was getting help, the emotion was feeling down or desperate, but I can't think about the action. I didn't take any action, did I?"

Yes, you did take action; you asked for help! You were humble enough to acknowledge that you needed help. You have no idea of how many people fail to ask for help, including you. You hardly ever ask for help. If you would ask more often, you would receive more help.

"So that's what happened?"

Yes, that's what happened. In this case, your emotions were very strong, and you were open-minded enough to see and understand the answer.

"I got exactly what I asked for; nothing more, nothing less."

That's right. It's important to carefully think about what you want, because if you're not clear on it, you can end up with something you don't want.

I know that you not only understand the concept but also put it in practice. Why don't you do that more often? You're completely in charge to create the life that you want. But I just have the feeling that you're still not convinced.

"No, I think I'm convinced."

Think?

"All right. I AM convinced, but… I find it hard to put it in practice. Or let's say that I find it hard to create the events I really want. Also, sometimes, it seems like nothing at all is happening, or it takes a very long time."

All it takes is practice. You'll see. And you know what they say about practice: sometimes you'll win and sometimes you'll fail, but only practice can make you win more often. Also, you're often caught up in the details of what you want…and that brings me to the second part of the answer on how to create great experiences. As for the timing of creation, depending on what you want to create, it manifests instantly or it can also take more time. But always trust that something will be happening.

So, back to your question: the first part of the answer was that you create by thought, intention, emotion, and action, and that you must ask for help if you want help.

The second part of the answer has to do with the plan for your life that was created before you were born.

"What!? What do you mean?"

Before you were born, you created a plan for your life, which included the people you'd meet and the things you would experience.

"Oh… But then it's all predetermined? My life is completely predetermined? If so, then it doesn't matter what I do, if I ask for help, or what choices I make. Are you saying that what was in the plan will actually happen without exception?"

No, not completely. What I'm saying is that there's a plan for your life about what you want to achieve, what your ultimate goal is. However, it doesn't say how you need to achieve it.

Let me try to explain: For example, you like hiking, and you would like to hike to the top of a mountain. So the plan is to reach the top. It doesn't say anything about how to get there or how long it must take. There are different paths you could take to get to the top, you may want to reach the top in one day, or you may want to take a week to get there. You really want to challenge yourself to take the most direct route, or you may take the longer easier way.

Another example is a project plan. A project plan gives you the timelines and the steps to reach your milestones and the ultimate goal as well as the resources/team members and others involved. However, it doesn't tell you how to do these steps, what methodologies to use, what tools to use, etc.

So the plan you set out before you were born sets out the end goal of your life and the lessons you want to learn, as well as the people who are there during your lifetime who will help you somehow to reach your goals and who will help you to learn your lessons.

"Okay, let's say that's all true, and I'm not saying it is, then what does this have to do with asking for help?"

You ask for help expecting a certain outcome, but that outcome may not be part of the big plan. It may not fit. When you ask for help, the help provided will be in accordance to the plan that, by the way, you created yourself with the help of others. When you ask for help, the help you'll (always) receive will be in accordance to the plan. So, if you ask for something that isn't in line with the plan, then the help you receive may not be the help you expected.

"Oh, wow… I need a moment to process this and understand it… But what you (me) are saying is that we all have a plan for our lives and we only have control of and make decisions about how we realize the plan? In other words, I have some control, but not completely?"

No, no, no. You have complete control. Remember that you created the plan. You carefully created the plan. And now you fulfil your plan, choosing the steps that lead to this fulfilment.

"Man, what bullshit I can come up with. How am I supposed to believe even what I write myself?"

Well, don't say it's bullshit, because it's not. Who do you believe puts those words in your head, and show them via your fingers typing this document?

"Hmm, it must be me…you?"

Yes, you who is me, who is part of All there is. You don't just come up with this. You know this because you're part of All there is. All parts of the All are connected. It's like a common unconsciousness in this physical form, while, on the other hand, there's a full common super creative consciousness connecting the whole parts of each individual in every form, time (as you call it), and place, creating the whole of All there is.

"Wow that's a mouth full! This is kind of new to me and reasonably mind blowing."

I can imagine it's a lot to take in, so give yourself time to let it sink in.

Reflection:

- **We often forget to ask for help, or are too stubborn or arrogant to ask for help.**
- **We're all responsible for anything and everything in our lives, because we create our own experiences.**
- **Ask and you shall receive.**
- **We all have a plan for our life.**

Not A Thousand Dresses

***

Another thing I need to raise with you is about what you really want, as you are often caught up in the details of that.

"Uhh?"

I said that you're often caught up in the details of what you want.

"What do you mean?"

You're often so caught up in the details of what you want that you're forgetting the bigger picture. You're forgetting what you REALLY want.

"You know what I really want?"

Of course, I do, and so do you.

"There are so many things I want. I want to have a great relationship with my partner, kids, and grandkids. I want to buy a nice house. I want a job I enjoy. I would like to drive a nice car. I would like to lose at least 20 kilos, I would like a thousand dresses (haha)."

NO, NO, NO, NO…

"What do you mean by NO?"

Stop thinking about details for a moment.

"Details? I thought these were pretty high-level desires."

Okay. Let me help you. If you could ask for one thing only, what would you really, really, really want? Think very carefully about your answer. If there's one dream, one wish that I could grant you, one thing that you could get, but nothing else, what would you ask for?

"Uhmm… Uhmm… That's hard. Only one thing? Really?"

Yes, only one thing.

"Then I guess I just want to be happy."

YES! PERFECT! That's a great answer! That's THE answer. Would you be happy if you had good health, plenty of money and in a great relationship? See, happiness implies all of that.

Let me explain by making a comparison with a GPS. You normally would only put your destination into your GPS. It already knows your current location.

And sometimes, you would also provide some conditions. For example, you only want to take roads without toll, you want to get to your destination the fastest way possible, you want the shortest route possible.

Then your GPS plots your route. This is the best possible route, given your conditions. Fantastic. You don't need to worry about how to get there. The GPS calculated all for you and will guide you road by road, corner to corner. Then off you go. You put your car in gear, push the accelerator then there you go. If you follow the instruction that the nice lady or man gives you, you'll surely arrive at your destination.

If you didn't know how to get to your destination, you wouldn't worry too much on how to get there, as long as you get there. You trust that the GPS will take you there.

Then when you're on your way, you realize that you left home without a coffee, and you really need one. You decide to make a detour. You know of this great coffee shop just about 2 kilometers further, but it will take you of your plotted course. As soon as you take a different road, the GPS starts recalculating and tries to get you back on the right track. But you ignore it, because you really, really need that coffee. All the way to the coffee shop, your GPS is recalculating.

You enjoy your coffee and then get into the car again. And guess what? Your GPS hasn't forgotten your destination. It just recalculates and gets you back on track. No matter how many detours you make, no matter how lengthy the detours are that you make, the final destination is never forgotten.

Your life is a bit like that. Your life is meant to drive you toward your plotted destination, no matter how many detours you make. You just have to keep your destination, your greatest wish in mind.

Can we break down that greatest wish into smaller ones? Yes, of course. These are the roads that take you there, or you could call it milestones.

So if you say that your ultimate wish is to be happy, then please keep this always in mind. You can have smaller wishes that together make you happy. For example, you may wish for great relationships, abundance, and good health. They all contribute to happiness.

Just don't get too attached to the details. There's no need. And if you get off track, the route to happiness will automatically be recalculated. Of course, you need to keep this end goal, your end destination in mind.

Guess what happens if you change your route, if you change your mind? Right. Your new route will be calculated! The universe is constantly working to get you to your destination. But there are an infinitive number of roads you could possibly take, and, sometimes, you decide to get distracted and put in a mini goal or wish on your way to the ultimate destination. The universe is constantly calculating and recalculating to get you there. The universe is always helping you.

The route you have in mind may not be the same route that the universe is calculating. You may want to go to the coffee shop west from the highway, although the universe has the coffee shop in mind that's just four km further, but that has better coffee. You may have set your mind on that fantastic job, but the universe may have a much better job in mind, which just takes a bit longer to get.

In other words, don't attach too much to the details. Keep the destination in mind, and I'll tell you...YOU WILL ARRIVE!

"Hmmm...okay...that sounds good...well kind of... I kind of understand. I just don't understand why there's so much suffering. If the universe works the way you're explaining, then how is it that most people never reach their destination?"

That's a fair question, and my answer is twofold: First, a lot of people mistake a pit stop for the destination. Second, if you can't see the complete picture, you'll be unable to determine what the real destination for other people is.

Also, depending on where you come from, a destination can look like a bad or a fantastic destination.

Let's talk about this a little bit more before we move on. Although it isn't my intention to explain life here, I'll explain a bit further. The intention is to help you understand what has happened in your life, and give you tools that can assist you dealing with the events that you call "bad."

Some people mistake a pit stop for the destination. For example, they believe that all that they want is to have that fantastic job that pays double of what they are earning right now. They may accept the job, but then find out that the people they have to work with really are not nice to work with, and there's no chance for any promotions in the future.

They believed that they needed this job to be happy. They may have been much happier with a lower paid job, working with great people, getting promotions and eventually earning much more. So, don't fret over details, but keep the ultimate goal in mind.

What I mean is that you'll be unable to determine what the real destination is for other people. You don't have the full picture, you cannot totally understand what other people are thinking or what their ultimate dream is, so don't judge. They're all en route but may have just stopped for a burger.

Also, what may appear as a bad destination to one person may be the ultimate destination to someone else.

And last but not least, who says that dying of starvation is the end destination for some people…?

"What you're saying is that I have to keep my ultimate destination in mind with all I do, and take baby steps to get there, trusting that the universe will help me get to that destination by recalculating and suggesting me to make a U-turn every time I derail?"

Yes, exactly that! And, also not to judge the journey of other people.

Everything hangs together and the universe always steers you in the right direction out of uncountable possibilities, even if it seems taking the long way or even the wrong way.

"So, I have to put my car into drive and press the accelerator? I have to take little steps toward my destination, but stop worrying about the route to take?"

That's it! Just let it go and take a step forward.

Now, there is another thing about this that I want to make clear.

I talked about how you make stops on your way. These are the mini goals or milestones. They are different from your end goal in the sense that they may not be constant.

"Oh, what do you mean?"

What I mean is this. Imagine that your end goal is to be happy, as we discussed before. Now if as a mini goal you choose to enjoy a nice cup of coffee, I want you to realize that as soon as you've finished your coffee and move on, then to enjoy this coffee is no longer a mini goal. If going on a nice trip is part of what makes you happy, then as soon as your trip has finished, it is no longer a goal.

The end goal of being happy will always stay the same, but the mini goals will come and go, just like you're driving toward a destination; the end will normally stay the same, but your mini-destinations will come and go. Mini destination can be a bathroom stop, a break for lunch, a stop to visit a nice lookout on the way, and so on.

These things are all important because they are on your way to your end goal. But don't get too hung up. What's most important is that you reach your end goal; in your case, it's that you're happy.

Your pit stops on the way to this end goal can change. They can change because you've reached them or because you changed your mind. Changing your mind about a pit stop or a mini goal happens normally because you obtained more information, which led to a different understanding and then to a different desire.

"Okay, I understand that I have to focus on the end goal, being happy, that there are mini goals or pit stops and that all I have to do is take the first step."

Yes, that's correct.

Reflection:

- We're often caught up in the details of what we want.
- What I really want is to be happy, because that suggests and includes great relationships, enough money, a good job, and good health.
- To reach our destination we only need to put on the GPS and push the accelerator.
- We often mistake a pit stop for our destination.
- Trust that your GPS will always get you back en route.

No Complaining

***

I'm just wondering…and, you probably don't want to hear this, but it seems to me that your life is actually pretty good.
Earlier you were complaining and complaining, but, so far, there doesn't seem too much to complain about.

"Well, you obviously don't know me at all. First, I'm not complaining. I'm merely stating the events in my life to try to make sense of all the things that have happened. We haven't even talked about the most painful events. I'm talking to you because I would like to heal all my pain and I can really use your help.

"I'm confused. I thought you were that part of me that knows, and yet, you talk as if I were just complaining. It isn't my intention to complain. My aim is to learn from my conversations with you. I need to learn in order to avoid the mistakes I've been making repeatedly. And yes, I'm in pain. Not in pain because of all the things that have happened. I'm in pain because I still don't seem to be healthy and have energy. Being always fatigued has an immense impact on my life. I just don't seem to be able to really build a comfortable life. I need your help in showing me what I've been doing wrong, and how I can change.

"I'm not complaining about the events in my life. No matter how painful. I've become a stronger and better person because of them. That doesn't mean I liked going through them and that doesn't mean I would like to continue having to go through events like that repeatedly. It simply means that I need to learn from my mistakes. Obviously, I haven't done that.

"I believed that you, the part of me that knows, could help me learn. Can you? Can you really help me, or am I just wasting my time here?"

I can help you and I'm already helping you. I'm merely testing and challenging you. I don't want you to lose sight of what you want to achieve by talking to me. I'm not saying you're complaining. I'm just saying to be careful not to start complaining, because then you'll forget the purpose of this whole conversation. I wouldn't want that to happen. Also, I need to remind you that, from time to time, quite a few events in your life have been very painful for you, but you chose them.

Another thing I want to talk to you about is self-confidence. I get some very mixed messages about this. Please tell me about your confidence or lack of it.

"All right, that, at least, is an easier subject. I have this memory of myself. I'm about four or five years old and I'm sitting at my desk in class at Kindergarten. We're singing songs, and I'm singing out loud without holding back. I love to sing. Singing makes me happy. Today I still remember that feeling of complete happiness, of complete confidence and enormous inner strength. It's actually amazing that I still remember that moment, but also amazing that at that very young age, I recognized that I was feeling so enormously happy and confident. Beautiful!

"Then, as I told you, a lot of things happened, and by the time I was about 16 years old, I had no confidence left at all. There was absolutely no confidence and no happiness. I felt unsure, shy, ugly, incompetent, and totally unhappy."

But that has changed now, hasn't it? What has made you a much happier and confident person today?

"Yes, it has changed. I'm much more confident now, and I'm a much, much happier person. Things have changed for the better, little by little. Partly because of other people, and partly because I've pushed myself to overcome my shyness and to overcome my fears of not being good enough.

"When I was 16 years old, I would have never thought that I could stand in front of a large room full of people and present something, without being scared or shy. My self-confidence has grown over the years, mainly over the last 10 to 15 years. When I was 16 years old, I would have never thought that I could be this happy and confident."

Do you have any idea how you increased your confidence?

"Well, it wasn't always easy, but for a long time I faked my confidence, until I truly became confident. You know the saying; Fake it until you make it. That really works. No kidding!

"With my increased confidence, I believe my happiness has also increased. My greatest happiness however comes from being around the people I love.

"I believe I have also come to appreciate the little things in life."

Can you explain what you mean by that?

"I mean, that I've come to understand that we don't, or I should say I don't need big things to make me happy. If you can find happiness in the little things, even if it's for a moment and you can find these little moments over and over again, then you can fill your life with little moments of happiness and you don't need to wait to find happiness in big things or happenings."

Can you give me an example of this?

"Sure. What I mean is that when you can stop for a moment and smell the roses, stop for a moment and really taste that great cup of coffee, stop for a moment and enjoy watching a child playing, stop for a moment and enjoy the laugh of a friend, a touch of a hand… If you're able to consciously enjoy that, then your life will be filled with little opportunities of happiness that can occur repeatedly in your life.

"In other words, you don't have to wait to win the lottery to be happy, you don't have to wait for that fantastic job to be happy, and you don't have to wait for that expensive car to be happy. Happiness can be just a touch or a smile away, if you choose to find it there."

Yes, well said. That's absolutely true. You don't have to wait for happiness.

You can find it right here and right now, like heaven on earth. Of course, there are all types of distractions that can tear you away. I hope though that you can remember your own words in those times that you feel unhappy.

So, for me to better understand; I hear you say that you first were happy and confident. Then because of certain events in your life, you became unhappy and no longer confident. Then, again, you became happy and confident, partly because you first faked it and also because you learned how to enjoy the little things in life that created this happiness and contentment.

"Yes, that's correct. Even though there may be things in my life that I don't like, as long as I consciously enjoy little good things, I can still live a very happy life. In this way, I can create my own happiness."

Reflection:

- Our life experiences make us stronger if we choose so.
- True happiness can be found in the smallest things.
- If you can find these little moments over and over again, then you can fill your life with little moments of happiness and you don't need to wait to find happiness in big things or happenings.
- You can find heaven on earth, here and now.

The Art Of Relating

***

I know that you're talking to me not only to get moving, to improve your situation, and make progress. You're also talking to me because you need help making sense of your pain. There's a lot of pain, hurt, trauma that needs to be dealt with. I know that this is what you want, but that you don't really want to ask for help with it. I know you feel stupid that you're not always able to deal with things yourself. I know that you won't bring up the subjects yourself; that's why I've decided to help you along and prompt you to talk about the things that have severely hurt you.

Let's talk about relationships. Tell me about it. What's your first thought when I say relationships?

"Pfft...Do we really have to? What's there to talk about? I've failed repeatedly and I don't know what I've been doing wrong.

"I'm in a very loving and caring relationship right now, but it took a very long time. I have been deeply hurt, several times, and this isn't something I really like to talk about. Can we talk about something else?"

Look, I know that this is painful for you, bringing up old pain. But there's a reason why we're talking here. Either you talk and try to make sense of it all with my help or you keep on asking questions like you always have.

You know, you can really be in a great relationship, and you're in a great relationship right now. You just need to understand why it hasn't always worked out for you. That way you can put the past behind you and really enjoy the great relationship you're in now. What do you say; do you want to try to sort things out and get more clarity?

"Okay, yes, you're right. I've been wondering many, many times why my relationships never seemed to be working out. I don't really feel like talking about it, but it's probably the only way to understand what's been going on each time."

All right then, let's go back to my question; What's your first thought when I say relationships?

"Betrayal, hurt."

Was there betrayal and hurt in all of your relationships?

"No, I've got a great relationship with my daughters, my sister, my father, and my husband."

So when you look at all these great relationships, can you think of anything they have in common?

"I thought about this question before and there are a few things that seem to stand out."

"First, I believe the good relationships in my life are all based on love, trust, and accepting each other for who we are. I never felt like I had to be someone else being with my daughters, sister, father, or husband. I've always felt relaxed with all of them. I always felt I could be myself with them.

They're all open-minded, loving, and kind hard-workers who are there for their family and friends. Also, they're honest people. They don't fake interest or betray people. They're people's people. Of course, they also make mistakes and don't always do the right thing, but I know they'll never hurt anyone on purpose. They all think about life, about other people, about nature, and about doing the best they can."

Exactly, these are the kind of people whom you should look for in your life. Do you know why?

"Uh, yes, because they're good people to whom I can relate?"

Yes, that's correct and also because they're like you and are more likely to understand you.

Now what about the relationships that went wrong, is there anything they have in common?

"The only thing I can think of is that they were all somehow depending on me. I wasn't depending on them, but they were depending on me. My mother, my ex-husband, my ex-partner, and my ex-business partner all in different ways were depending on me. And I know that, at work, some of my managers were afraid that I'd go after their jobs, so I didn't always get a deserved promotion. They felt threatened by me and my knowledge.

"And there's something else… But I'm not sure if this really has to do with relationships."

What is it?

"It's about the female and male role."

What about it?

"I feel, sometimes, that through my experiences, I've been forced to take on more of the male role than the female role."

Okay, we're going a bit off track here, but can you explain that?

"When you look at the traditional male role, and I'm over-generalizing here, you can say that they work, bring the money in, do repairs around the house, make the main decisions, and take care of the big things that need to be organized. A man also is considered to be the stronger one.

"When I think of the traditional female role, I think about having the primary care of the children, cooking, cleaning, and taking care of other family members. A woman is thought to be the caring, kind and loving one."

True, that's probably a rough outline of the old traditional male and female role. But I'm not sure if I understand your point here.

"It's not really a point, it's a feeling that I've had for a while. I feel that I've been forced to take on more of the male role, which came at the cost of playing less of the female role."

Can you explain that?

"In two of the relationships that I've had, I always felt that I had to be the stronger person. Most of the time, I had to provide the main income, I was the main or only provider for the family. I was also the one organizing everything and having to make the main decisions. In having to do so, I feel like I've missed out in seeing my kids grow up. I've never seen their first steps, heard there first words. Things like that…. I'm not sure how to explain this. I feel as if I had to take on both roles, and because I had to do so, I've missed out on some of the parts of a traditional female role.

"I've always felt like I had to take care of everything and everyone. I feel like I've always been there taking care of others and no one has ever taken care of me. That hurts. Apart from now being with my husband, it feels like that whatever happened, I was always on my own. I didn't need to expect any help from anyone. It was my experience that I was never getting any help. It was my experience that no one ever would take care of me. I was always battling on my own. I had no support whatsoever. That's painful, lonely, and exhausting.

"I know that my dad took care of me as much as he could. I also know my sister will always be there for me, but she's overseas and also has been through bad times when I knew she needed all her energy for herself and her family.

"I also know that now that my daughters are older, they'll take care of me as much I'll take care of them. I have no doubts about that. Things have certainly changed, but it's been a very hard time in the past."

I understand, and I know that you're hurt and tired of trying repeatedly, hoping that someone will be there for you as much as you're there for others. Today, though, you're in a very loving and caring relationship with someone who truly cares and does take care of you, and there are your daughters and sister too who love you very much, and they too will take care of you and have been taking care of you when you needed their support.

But here too, there's something that you need to learn.

Something that's really hard for you. Something that's very understandable, though, considering your experiences in life. One of the things you need to learn is to ask for help!

"Oh, but I do ask for help."

Really?

"Yes."

Are you sure?

"What? Do you doubt me? I do ask for help. It's just that I hardly ever receive any help."

Really?

"Stop saying really! It's annoying. I KNOW I ask for help."

Yes, you do ask for help...sometimes...when it's too late. And most of the times, you don't really ask for what you really need.

"Oh, really?"

No need to get sarcastic again. See, again, you're hearing something you don't like. Do you understand why you hardly ever ask for help?

"No?"

I could say "really?" again, but instead I'll help you a little bit, although you're probably not going to like what you're hearing. You hardly ever ask for help because you feel unworthy.

Did you hear that? Let me repeat that because it's very important.

You hardly ever ask for help because you feel unworthy!

"Hmmm. I don't like what you're suggesting, but if I'm honest, I'll have to admit that you're probably right. I probably did feel unworthy in the past. I think that has changed over time, but yes, there are still times that I feel unworthy. I definitely feel stupid to have to ask for help. It makes me feel like I'm not good enough. Well, I often feel like I'm not good enough. I know I've built up this cocoon of self-confidence, but, deep in my heart, I sometimes still feel that I'm not good enough. That's the reason why I find it so hard to ask for help."

You're spot on there. And I know you think that you're stupid for asking for help. But it's caused by a pattern in your life and it really isn't your fault. It has been created through different negative experiences in your life when you were told that you weren't good enough.

We need to look at this a bit deeper to understand what has happened and to turn this feeling around in an appropriate self-confidence about who you are.

To do that, we'll need to have a look at your experiences in life and your relationships, especially that one with your mother. That relationship has been the building block for the other relationships in your life. It will clarify a lot of things in your life that you're not able to understand or turn around at this time.

Are you willing to do that? It will probably be the hardest part of our conversation and it will bring back painful memories, but, in my opinion, it will bring more clarity and understanding and a chance to change your future relationships. What do you say?

"This is going to be hell. I don't like to talk about my mother. She's hurt me so much. But I do get your point. Is it okay that when we do that, to give me the opportunity to end our conversation at any time it becomes too overwhelming and pick it up another time? I'm not sure if I'm able to work through this is one go."

That's fine. It will be impossible to work through your relationships in one go. There's too much and you'll also need time to adjust your thinking.

Now, before we start talking about your mother, I want to dig a little bit deeper into the concept of relationships. Can you tell me what you believe are the aspects of a great relationship?

"I think, for me, two things stand out. There has to be mutual trust, and I believe you can only be in a great relationship if you can be yourself and allow the other person to be him or herself as well. So, in other words, not trying to change the other person, but rather accepting the other one for who he or she is. Obviously, this needs to come from both sides.

"An obvious aspect and connection to that is communication. It's so important to truly communicate with each other."

Can you see how real communication is only possible if there is mutual trust?

"Uh, I think I can, but can you please explain?"

To reap the benefits of good communication, you have to trust that the other person accepts you for who you are, and truly listens to what you have to say, and then, in return, they have to communicate back with the same trust. If you talk to someone you don't really trust, you may not say what you'd really like to say, simply because you feel that that other person will not accept it or not accept you. Good communication is based on trust, honesty, mutual interest, and the ability and willingness to truly listen to one another.

"Yes, that's exactly what I mean. That for me is another important aspect of a good relationship."

Reflection:

- **Find people who love, trust and accept you for who you really are.**
- **You'll feel most comfortable with people who are more like you.**
- **Love yourself first. Only then can others love you too.**

A Golden Cage

***

We'll be talking about your other relationships as well, but to start with, can you tell me about your relationship with your mother? This is something really big.

"Honestly, I wouldn't know where to start. When I think of her, I still feel cold, abandoned, betrayed, and unloved.

"Yes, I've finally been able to forgive her, but that doesn't mean I suddenly feel loved or that I don't feel abandoned and betrayed by her.

"I have this picture in my mind of how a mother should be: loving, nurturing, caring, kind, and warm. Unfortunately, that's nothing like my mother.

"I used to be scared of her. It was as if I could never do anything good, as if I were to blame for all that went wrong. I felt like it always was me causing the issues in her life. I always felt stupid and ugly. She always told me I was stupid and ugly. I certainly don't have a lot of good memories.

"I'd be lying if I said it was all bad. Of course, that isn't true. Things are never that black and white. But, for me, the bad times, the lies, the manipulations, the pain doesn't weigh up to the good times."

Has that always been like that or did you have a time with your mother that you did feel loved?

"I don't know. I always felt scared of my mother. I always felt that if I didn't please her, she wouldn't love me. She always made me feel that I wasn't good enough. There was this sinking feeling when I was around her, this pit in my stomach that would never go away.

"The first time I realized that, it must have been when I was about 6 years old. I had started primary school and I loved it. I was very eager to learn and always trying to do the best I could. I think by that time I'd already learned that in order to be loved by my mother, I had to be really good not only as a student but also as a human being. I had to be perfect! Even at that young age, it was already exhausting to try to live up to her standards.

"That first year at school, I was sick for about three quarters of the time, which, of course, isn't a real good thing for the first year of your learning life when the foundations of language and math are being laid down. I had about all the child diseases you can imagine and was also hospitalized two times. To be honest, I don't remember too much about being always sick. The first time in hospital, my tonsils were taken out, and the second time, I had a colic of my intestines."

How did that made you feel, being in hospital, without your family? It must have been hard, considering you were so young.

"The first time with my tonsils was like an adventure. Yes, I was in a bit of pain, but not too much. And after they had been taken out, I was given an ice stick to suck on. It wasn't so bad and I think I was back home the next day.

"The second time when I had the colic was very different. I felt very alone. I was in hospital for about a week and my sister wasn't allowed to come in and visit me. I really missed her. I think the worst thing was feeling humiliated. I had my own room, but there was a glass wall between the other room. And because I had severe constipation, I had to sit on the potty on my bed in plain sight of the child who was in the other room. I also remembered the nurses being angry with me because I couldn't poo. They told me I couldn't go home unless I was able to."

You felt humiliated.

Yes, I did. I felt I was on public display. I also felt like the nurses were blaming me for being constipated. They weren't very nice.

"Being away from home didn't bother me, except for not being able to see my sister. My sister and I were very close, and not being able to see her was very hard for me. I truly missed her.

"Back at school, I remember having an average of about 70% at the end of that first year and my mother was very disappointed in me. She expected a lot better from me."

> *How did you know that she was expecting more? You were only 6 years old. How come you think that she was disappointed?*

"I remember she told me that she'd expected me to have at least between 80 and 90%, preferably more even. And she told me that some other children in my class did a lot better than I did. I still remember because I was so sad. I'd worked really hard to keep up with the class even though I had been sick. And I was happy with what I'd done. Yes, I wasn't the best in class, but considering all, I thought I'd done pretty well. It was a pretty hard time for me. I felt so much pressure already at such a young age."

> *Okay, yes, I know it was a pretty hard time for you. Was there anything else that happened around that time that had a big impact on you?*

"Uh, kind of…"

> *So?*

"So what?"

> *Are you going to talk about it?*

"It's a bit strange."

> *Yes?*

"Okay, then… When I was a little bit younger than that, when I was about 4 or 5 years old, I used to see ghosts or spirits coming through the wall of my bedroom.

"I was so scared and would try to hide under my blankets. I cried and screamed and then my parents would come. They thought I was making it all up, since they couldn't see anything or anyone, but I know they were there. I could see them and I was afraid. I always felt like they were trying to harm me. I had trouble sleeping. It was as if they were trying to hit me with their fists. There were many spirits and their fists where coming through the wall. I still vividly remember today."

What happened, are they still coming?

"No, they're no longer coming, or, at least, I'm not aware of it. One night, when I was about to go to sleep, they appeared again through the wall and I was upset and became more and more scared. Then I got really angry at them. I told them to go away and stay away. I told them that I was no longer afraid and that I would hit them if they ever dared to come back. It's funny that I still remember how angry and how determined I was to get rid of them, even at that young age. After that one night, I never saw them again."

How did you feel after that?

"I felt very strong and confident. They never came back. I think I'd scared them off. I was kind of proud of myself. No one believed me and came to help me. I had to fight them by myself and I did it!

"It was probably the first time that I realized I couldn't always count on other people, even my parents. I think a part of me at that time started to understand that I wasn't really protected and understood. It felt like the home I lived in wasn't that warm safe haven I thought it was. The good thing was that I'd learned to stand up for myself."

I remember that moment. You tapped into the part of you that's me. Although you were still very young, you found a way to access the whole you. Children always do that a lot easier than adults do. They're more open to what adults believe to be weird or strange or even impossible.

You were a very intuitive child who simply felt things, knew things. Now that you're older, you often don't use that part of you anymore. It's still there, but it needs practice, it needs to be used to benefit you and to help you live a more wholesome life. It would also help you to help others. There are moments that it's there in your live, very obviously. You know what moments I'm talking about.

I know that you believe you seem to KNOW things and sometimes to FEEL, SEE, or HEAR things. You do, even though you tend to doubt yourself.

You're still very intuitive, and if you would simply relax more and be calm inside, you'd find yourself having these moments a lot more than you're having them now.

I know you also know that your mother also sees and feels things.

"Yes, that's true. However, she never wants to talk about it. I don't know. It looks to me like she is scared of it."

What about the other thing that happened around this time?

"I don't know what you're talking about. What do you mean? Was there something else that happened?"

Yes there was. Something really big, that you've been pushing away. I know you're thinking about it right now. I also know that you don't really want to talk about it. You think it's so out of the ordinary that no one would believe you. You're actually a bit scared that it may be true, and you wouldn't know how to deal with that. That's why you don't want to talk about it.

I understand that. But in order to really benefit from our conversation, you should really open up and talk about it. It has had such a big effect on your life that it's time to understand more about what actually happened.

"Sorry, but I still don't know what you're talking about."

Yes, you do know. I understand that you're scared, but I also know you well enough that you would like to get it out in the open.

"Maybe… But not now. I'm not ready. Anyway, memories of this only came back when I was in my thirties. Just after the time it happened, it was as if all my memories were gone. To be honest I'm not even sure it really happened. Maybe I'm making it all up. Maybe I just have a huge imagination."

Really?

"Maybe."

No.

"No, what?"

No, you're not making it up. You know you're not making it up. But I have to agree, it would be much easier on you if you had made it up. But no, you didn't. It's all real. It doesn't matter how out of the ordinary or strange it is; it did really happen.

But okay, we'll leave it for now. However, be assured I'll get back to it later.

"We'll see."

Now, let's get back to where we left off. Apart from this event that you'll be talking about later, what else happened?

Something related to your mother that explains your feeling toward her. I know that there's one thing that has destroyed all the faith and all the trust that you had in your mother.

What happened?

"I must have been nine years old and I was at school in this class with a terrible teacher who would hit his pupils and constantly swear. This would happen on a daily basis.

"When I told my mother, she was very shocked. She told me to come home if it would ever happen again. I said to her that that wasn't going to be easy. I couldn't just walk out of the classroom, could I? My mother told me to go to the bathroom instead, and then sneak out and come home. So, the next time the teacher hit one of the students, I went to the bathroom and then sneaked out of the school building to go home.

"I thought I'd done the right thing, but when I got home my mother was upset and angry with me and had a real go at me. She made me apologize to the teacher. I didn't understand any of it. I thought that I had to come home, but now my mother blamed me and made me feel stupid in front of the teacher and the other kids. I felt very confused and stupid.

"The teacher was angry with me and the other children in the class thought it just was not right to go home. They started to bully me. My mother had let me down. I felt really betrayed. I hadn't done anything wrong. I'd just listened to her like a good girl, but now I was bullied at school. My mother and the teacher made me feel like I had done something bad. I hadn't really done anything bad at all. I was just a little girl who had listened to her mom and who was now made a fool of.

It had upset me so much that I got sick and my parents transferred me to another school. Of course, at this school, all the teachers knew about what had happened. I felt like I was looked at and found guilty. I lost all my self-confidence and all my happiness. All my spontaneity, my joy had disappeared. I was nowhere near being a happy child. I felt incredibly stupid and guilty for something I had been told to do by my mother."

Yes, you were deeply hurt and it took a very long time to get over it, if you really ever got over it at all. Why do you think your mother betrayed you and didn't back you up?

"Well, the only thing I understand about my mother is that she's scared about what others may say. It all has to look perfect on the outside. And as long as it all looks perfect on the outside, it doesn't matter to her who gets hurt or how it really is on the inside.

"I believe she didn't want to admit that she had told me to come home. That would have made her look bad and she would have needed to defend herself for making that decision. It was a lot easier to blame me because, in the end, I was the one who went home, and I was just a stupid little girl.

"It also almost looks as if this event was the trigger for her to treat me as if I didn't matter. After this, time after time, she'd make me apologize for things I'd never done. She would try to manipulate me and make a fool of me in public. She also tried to come in between my sister and me. I think that after the school incident, I never really trusted her again.

"The thing is that I tried so hard to make her love me. I did everything to please her just to get a little bit of love. But whatever I did, it was never good enough. I was never good enough. And now, I finally understand that whatever I do, I'll never be good enough in her eyes."

I know that your mother gave you the feeling and even told you that you weren't good enough. Do you still feel that you're not good enough?

"Oh, she still does give me that feeling. The difference is that I now know that I'm a good person and that I try the best that I can. Sure, I'm not perfect, but no one is. But I believe I can honestly say that I'm a good person.

"I don't think that my mother can agree with that. I may be a good person, but I'm not good enough. I actually think that she's ashamed of me. She probably was ashamed of me after the school incident. Not that she had any reason to be ashamed. But hey, it's probably easier to be ashamed of me than take some accountability herself."

Tell me about other occasions where you mother really hurt you.

"Well, there was this time… I'm not sure if she really hurt me, but she did get me into a difficult situation.

"When I was about 11 years old, my grandfather from my dad's side passed away. For some reason, my dad's family was angry at my mother about something that had happened around that time. I still don't know what had actually happened, but my mother and my dad's families were having arguments. And I wasn't allowed to see my grandmother anymore. That was very difficult for me. My grandmother was more a mother to me than my own mother had ever been. I trusted her and loved her and I could always feel that she loved me too. Now, I wasn't allowed to see her anymore. I felt really bad about it because I loved her very much.

"It wasn't until I was 18 years old that my mother and my dad's family made up. Well, kind of…. I was allowed to see my grandmother again, but my mother made it very clear that she didn't want me going.

"So I felt torn apart. I felt like I had let my grandmother down for all those years and didn't feel at ease anymore when I would visit her now. I felt guilty that I never visited her secretly. But whenever I did visit her now, I also felt like I let my mother down. I knew my mother still couldn't stand my grandmother and that she didn't want me to go.

"It's a shame. My grandmother was one of the very few people who made me feel accepted, and who made me feel happy and good about myself and I had lost her. I know it wasn't completely my mother's fault, I understand that it wasn't something she did to hurt me, but it did hurt me after all. I was caught in the middle of a fight that I didn't want to be part of.

"That I did want to see my grandmother just didn't matter. My opinion didn't ever matter. You know how it is; a good girl listens to her mom."

I know that that was very difficult for you, that you missed your grandmother very much, and that you felt very guilty. If there's anything you could say to your grandmother right now, what would it be?

"I would say, 'I'm sorry Oma, I'm sorry I didn't come to visit you. I'm sorry we lost out on times that we could have enjoyed each other's company. I'm sorry I let you down. I know it wasn't my fault, and that I was just trying to be a good girl and listen to my mother, but I really am sorry. I want you to know that I love you very much, that I cherish all the moments we spent, and that I'll never forget you.'"

Good. I'm sure she'd be happy to hear that. I'm also sure she'd say the same to you! She loves you very much.

Now, tell me what happened that drove you into a downwards spiral. Up to now, you were a hurt child with not a lot of self-confidence, but things got a lot worse.

"When I was 16, I met someone when we were on holidays in Italy. We were very much in love, but my parents didn't agree. I don't think the problem was that he was Italian. I believe the problem was that he was a guy. I don't think that anyone would have been okay to be my boyfriend or my friend at all.

"My mother always had comments about all my friends: too fat, too skinny, too poor, too rich, not reformed, or not religious at all, black skin, not from the Netherlands, and so on. My mother always had something negative to say about my friends or their family.

"Anyway, I was madly in love with him. And when I was back home in the Netherlands, he sent me a letter and a beautiful bracelet with an inscription. But when I came home from school, my mother had already unpacked the package and had opened and read the letter."

Wait! Are you saying that your mother opened your mail?

"Yes, she did. She always did. There was no privacy at all. I remember one day, my mother went to my sister's room and read her journal. I'll never forget that. I thought it was sneaky and mean. So, she didn't just go through my mail, but also went through private things in my room or my sister's room.

"My best friend from school was with me at that time. My mother was really angry and ordered me to send it all back and tell him that I didn't want him to contact me any longer. To my friend, she said that she couldn't understand how anyone could be interested in someone as ugly as me. And how could I even fall in love with someone in Italy?"

You must have been very upset. Were you angry with your mother?

"No, I wasn't angry. I felt very sad, but I thought that my mother was right, that I didn't deserve to be loved.

"Years later, I heard from my friend that she had been very shocked. She'd seen and heard other things at our place that she didn't like, but the way my mother had treated me that time was so very wrong, and she never forgot it. She asked her parents if I could come and live with them. She believed I shouldn't live with my mother."

How did you feel?

"At that time, I felt really stupid and unworthy of someone to love me. I thought my mother was right and that I was ugly and stupid. By that time, she had manipulated and hurt me enough for me to believe she was right and I was wrong. I truly believed I was the ugliest and most stupid girl on earth and that I didn't have the right to even believe that someone could love me or care for me.

"I only learned much later from my friend, that she had asked her parents if I could come and live with them. I wished I had known at that time that she knew how I was treated by my mother and that she didn't agree. It could have made a difference at the time just knowing that someone was on my side. But nevertheless, it was a nice thing to hear years later.

"It came to a point that I was very withdrawn. I hated to have to go to school, and I would sit at the back of the class. I was the grey mouse sitting at the back of the class who would turn red every time someone would try to have a conversation.

"At the same time, my grades went down. I went from scoring between 80 and 100% to scoring between 30 and 50% for all subjects, especially math.

"My mother was checking and testing all my homework and would make me go back to my room and study if I even made one single mistake when she was testing me. Every school day, I would get up at 6.30am, go to school, and then come home and study till 10.30pm. On Saturdays, I'd get up at the same time to hop on my bike at 7 am to get extra math tutoring. Sundays were for church and studying."

What effect did that have on you?

"Looking back, I think I just burned out by the time I was 16. I was so tired! I was tired and felt very down on myself. I was constantly sick as well. I would always at least have a cold and very often a sinus infection.

"One day, I had a meeting with my math teacher and my class mentor. I remember being so shy. I didn't know why my results had dropped so much. I felt so stupid, so low, so depressed. After the meeting, my class mentor said to me that he thought I was socially awkward. And that I should really work on my social skills. I was so hurt. Yes, maybe he was right, but he didn't need to say it that way. He didn't even try to find out why.

"When I was 18, I failed my final exams and had to repeat the year. I had to spend another year at school in a year when I didn't know any of the other kids. I hated it! There were two other girls I could talk to, but they didn't always attend the same classes. I felt pretty lonely. But I did pass the second time. Just. I only just passed all my exams, nothing more, nothing less.

"I know my mother then wanted me to go to university. That would look good because no one in the family had been to university. But I wasn't up for it. I had had enough of studying. I wanted to do something for me, something that I would really like. I ended up doing a year at an international hostess school, where French was the second language."

So, your mother wanted you to get a university degree? That isn't such a bad thing.

"No, it isn't a bad thing at all, but after all my failures at school, and the long hours of studying, I felt like I would never be able to go to university. I felt like I was just not smart enough. I was also very tired. Exhausted, that's how I felt.

"After I'd failed my exam the year before, I went to Switzerland to work in a café/restaurant during my school break. It was in the French speaking part of Switzerland. And, although it was pretty hard in the beginning, after 3 weeks, I managed very well and was given a lot of responsibility at work. I loved it and it gave me some of my self-confidence back. See, I wasn't that stupid. I survived working in another country, speaking another language, and I was doing really well and made a lot of friends in a very short time. I was so happy and felt so good about myself.

"So this French school seemed to be a good choice. And it was. I absolutely loved it. It was a lot of study, but all subjects I enjoyed doing. And at the end of the year, I had to go to France for work experience in a Novotel."

So, you were going to another country again? Do you think you were escaping from home?

"Looking back, yes, I think I did. Of course, not the first time when I went to Switzerland. I had no idea how it would turn out, and, to be honest, it was a bit scary at first. But yes, I was very happy to go back when they asked me to come and work during my other school holidays.

"For the hostess school, we were meant to do our work experience in a different country. It was just part of the curriculum, but something that I sure did welcome. Anyway, it was just for 6 weeks.

"I loved the buzz of going somewhere I had never been before, I loved to see how I could cope with having to speak a different language, how I'd adapt to a different country with different customs. I think I loved going to Switzerland and France because, although it was a challenge, it gave me something positive in my life. It also gave me self-confidence and the feeling that I wasn't completely worthless.

"Working in that Novotel in France was so much fun. The people were great. They would ask me to go out with them all the time. They really gave me the feeling that I was someone, that they accepted me, that I was good enough to hang out with. I had the feeling that I belonged, which was something I had never experienced before.

"I remember that during the weekend I would work up to midnight and then go out with some of the other staff. We would dance and party all night and then around 5 am have breakfast, go back to have a shower and start work at 7 am. That was exhausting, but lots of fun."

But that time in France wasn't all fun, was it? Something happened that hurt you to the core of your being.

"No, it wasn't all fun. Something was taken away from me that was very dear."

What was it?

"My dog was taken away. It still hurts really deeply and thinking of it still brings tears to my eyes. He was the one to comfort me in all those hours when I felt sad, when I felt stupid and ugly. It was as if he were the only one who understood me. He was the only one to give me love and positive attention. My dog was my best friend. It felt that he was the only one I could really count on."

Why was he taken away from you?

"During my time in France I received a letter from my mother. I'll never forget, because it was on my 20th birthday. Earlier that day she had called me to wish me a happy birthday, but she hadn't mentioned Arpad at all.

"Then, later that day, I received a letter from her, telling me that she had sold our dog. When I called her and questioned her about it, she told me that she was allergic to the dog and that he had to go. That's one of my mother's favorite common excuses, being allergic. Never, ever before had she complained about being allergic to the dog. And I honestly didn't believe her. I think she believed it was too much trouble to take care of him. And not one single moment she thought of asking me for my opinion. If it had been really true about her being allergic, I would have moved out and taken the dog. I'd almost finished my year and was about to look for a job. But I didn't even get the chance to do that.

"My mother just got rid of the dog without even thinking that I might want to keep Arpad or at least have a chance to say goodbye. Up to today, seeing a dog like Arpad brings tears to my eyes. I always wonder what happened to him and if he was happy. Even writing this down here right now really upsets me.

"My mother took away the only thing that kept me going, the only one who loved me. I still find it very hard to deal with. My family doesn't understand that. They think I'm egoistic. But I'm sure that anyone who has a pet and loves it can understand that it deeply hurts when it's just taken away from you without even having a chance to say goodbye."

It seems to me that you had to put up with a lot of grief from your mother, and, at some point in your life, you had enough of it. Tell me about that time.

"Something happened that made me realize that she'd never love me and that no matter how hard I would try, she'd never be a real mother to me.

"At that time, I was already living in Australia, and I went through a really hard time, having no work and no money. I was trying to live on 25-30 Australian dollars each week to buy groceries for myself, my two daughters and another teenage girl whom I was taking care of. I didn't even have money for a $5 school field trip and no money for new shoes for one of my girls, who was wearing shoes with holes and was getting wet feet every time it rained.

"I put away all my pride and asked my mother in the Netherlands, if she could send me 100 dollars, so I could buy new shoes for my daughter and buy something decent to eat. My girls didn't know, but I often went to bed on an empty stomach, and was skipping meals because there simply wasn't enough to eat.

"My mother told me that she didn't have $100 because she was about to redecorate her bedrooms. She hadn't done that in a few years and it was really time to do so because she was allergic to the floor cover in one of the spare rooms. Then she sent money to one of my daughters and told her to buy a food processor.

"For me, that was the last straw. What mother would let her daughter and grandchildren starve, but then send money for a food processor? I felt strongly that my mother only lived for herself and for what others might say or think. Everything had to be perfect on the outside for her. She had to pretend that everything was perfect all the time. Everything had to be clean, all had to be in the right place, her kids had to be perfect and successful. Perfect, perfect, perfect. Pffft.

"At the same time, she was volunteering and sending food to Romania. Again, that looked absolutely great on the outside. Of course, no one knew that she was letting her own family starve.

"To me, that was really it. Something snapped inside of me. My mother would never ever love me or care for me. No matter what I would do, no matter how hard I'd been fighting for her love, I would never be good enough for her. The way my mother treated me, suddenly made me realize that I could never change her. It also made me realize that I was sick of having to put up with her. I'd had enough of her. I was way better off without her.

"I wrote her a letter explaining why I no longer wanted to have contact with her. She refused to give me any kind of reaction and acted as if nothing were wrong.

"I was absolutely fed up with her abuse! I felt it was up to her to fix our relationship if she wanted to do that. She needed to take the first step. I wanted to have some kind of acknowledgement of what she had done. I didn't even need a real apology. I just wanted my pain to be acknowledged. I wanted her to validate me, if that makes any sense. But knowing her, I didn't feel that that would ever happen. I had lost all my respect for her, or maybe I should say that I had lost the last little bit of respect that was left."

Well, it's really clear what you thought of your mother, and with good reason. So, what do you believes she thinks about you?

"Honestly, I don't care anymore what she thinks about me. I'm past that. I know her thinking about me has never been very positive. She probably thinks I'm stupid, stubborn, a loser, and God knows what else."

And...is she right?

"Oh, I'm definitely stubborn. But I actually think it's not always such a bad thing. The Dutch word for stubborn is 'eigenwijs'. This is actually two words in one: 'eigen' en 'wijs,' which translated into English actually means 'own wise,' 'own way,' or also 'own song.' To me, that sounds good. If I look at those words, it would mean that I use my own wisdom, go my own way, or sing my own song. To me those aren't necessarily negative things, they are more signs of strength.

"I know I'm a bit stubborn but I'm always willing to listen to advice. In the end, though, I'll also always make my own decision. I think that's the part that isn't appreciated by my mother. I believe that she always wanted me to follow her advice, do what she wanted me to do, be the person she wanted me to be. But I couldn't be the person that she wanted me to be. I can only be me.

"The other things…no, I'm far from stupid and I'm definitely not a loser. I think my mother believes that, because I'm not doing what she wants me to do.

"Others have called me a woman with balls, superwoman, and a hero. I probably am a woman with balls, not that I really have balls, but I've done things that require balls. That requires an attitude of 'just do it,' no complaining but taking a (calculated) risk and working and aiming toward a positive outcome.

"And, yes, at times, I may have thought of myself as being superwoman. Not that I'm that great, but I push myself pretty hard. I always push the boundaries, my boundaries and sometimes I cross my own limits, believing that I'm super woman and that I can actually do it. Sometimes, I push myself so hard that I have to find out the hard way that I can only go so far. I do go over my limits at times, and I don't think that's necessarily a bad thing. I always say that whenever I go over my limits and I'm still breathing and kicking, it actually shows that my real limits are much higher than I thought they were.

"I've also been called a hero. That's a title I surely don't deserve. I'm not a hero. I've never done anything heroic. I'm just a simple country girl, with simple wishes and dreams."

"But yes, I believe my mother thinks I'm stupid, she believes I never listen to her, and she doesn't agree with the choices I've made in my life."

Do you have any idea of what has caused her behavior toward you? I think it's important that you give that serious thought.

"I believe there are a few factors here. First, she's afraid of what other people may say. So for her it's really important that all looks great on the outside. It almost looks like an obsession. It doesn't matter if she hurts her own family or other people, as long as it all looks good.

"She is obsessively neat. All has to be clean and tidy and she used to check if I'd dusted and cleaned. For her, cleaning is more important than spending time together, more important than relaxing. In a way I understand; it's not like she had much else to do. My mother has never really worked, except for 2 or 3 years when she just left school, and for a short while in a part-time nursery job. I suppose that cleaning was partly a way of spending her time. As long as everything was clean and as long as our family did everything right, my mother was happy. There was no room for mistakes or failure, especially not from me. I think my being her first child, she projected all her life expectations on to me. From the outside, I believe we always looked like a happy little family. I don't believe a lot of people actually knew what was going on.

"The other reason may be that she didn't have a happy childhood herself. She wasn't given the opportunity to study, which was something she really wanted to do. I believe she projected all her dreams and expectations onto me. She wanted me to have and do what she wasn't able to have and do. I can understand that. The thing is that she took it too far. She forgot that I wasn't her and that I didn't have the same dreams.

"Also, my mother was physically and emotionally abused by her mother. I suppose when this happens, you either copy this type of behavior in your own life, or you do the exact opposite. I understand that on her side of the family, there had been abuse for many generations.

"I believe she used anything possible to create her own little world without imperfections and she wasn't shy to use lies and manipulation to achieve that. I'm not saying she necessarily is a bad person. She just isn't the kind of person I want to be associated with. Unfortunately, she's my mother, so I had to put up with her."

Are there any positive things about your mother? It looks like it's all bad, but no one is just only bad. So is there anything that you learned or that you admired?

"Sure, there certainly are a few things that stand out in a more positive way. I inherited her love for languages. Whenever we would go on a holiday and cross the border, my mother would have a little book with words and phrases in German, French, Italian, or Spanish. She would really make an effort to address people in their own language.

"That has definitely sparked my interest in other languages as well. I'm not a natural, and I really have to put in a lot of effort to learn a different language, but I enjoy trying to speak to people in their own language.

"My mother is also very creative. Not just with her hands, but she also enjoys writing. So, guess where my love for writing comes from?

"What I admire as well is that she got her driving license some years after my dad passed away when she was already in her mid-fifties."

That's great. At least you can also see some positive things in your mother. How do you feel about the abuse and the negative behavior now?

"Well, I can't live her life for her. She has to realize that I'm not her, that I'm a separate person, and that I have my own dreams and need to follow my own path. That includes making my own mistakes.

"Like I've said before, I've lost the last little bit of respect that I had for my mother. It's gone. I realized that I would never want to have a 'friend' like her. I wouldn't trust her. I wouldn't want to have anything to do with her. I didn't want to have to do anything with her even though she's my mother.

"The thing is that she's never been a real mother to me. She's never been there for me. It didn't matter how hard I tried to please her. I was and I probably will never be good enough.

"And I deserved to be treated a lot better than that. I didn't deserve the way she treated me. I wouldn't accept that kind of behavior from a friend. And after having had to put up with this kind of behavior from my mother for over 40 years, I decided that I didn't want to have to put up with this any longer.

"I decided that unless she was able to change (and I couldn't see that happening), I didn't want anything to do with her. She has been a really negative factor in my life. And I simply wanted that to stop. She has dragged me down, made a fool of me, took away my self-confidence, and betrayed me repeatedly. That's over now. That isn't going to happen again. I understand that she's never going to change. Therefore, I had to take care of myself by cutting off all contact with her. It isn't that I hate her. It's that I never want to be hurt by her ever again."

Reflection:

- Trying to live up to other people's expectations will tire you out and make you unhappy.
- You're always good enough, no matter what other people say.
- You cannot blame others for not understanding you, as we all have different experiences and different truths.
- True love travels beyond the grave.
- Always be your own person and follow your own way, without intentionally hurting other people.
- Make your own decisions, but also take full responsibility for them.

The Wonder Of Forgiveness

***

But something did change didn't it?

"Yes, something did change. You're right. Being a mother myself, I still don't understand how a mother could treat her child the way my mother treated me, but, somehow, I've found it inside of me to forgive her."

Tell me what happened?

"I'm not sure what happened... I've thought about it many times, but I'm not really sure what happened."

I think you do know what caused you to forgive your mother. But you believe it's a little strange.

"Okay, yes, you're right. It is strange, as it just happened without any extra thought or effort from my side. Where do I start?

"When my older daughter got married, my mother came over to visit them, staying for six weeks. And, of course, in that time, I did see her two or three times. At that time, nothing had really changed. I had no desire to see her or to talk to her. To be honest, I just wanted her to stay away. I'd rather not see her ever again.

"Then she came over again when my other daughter got married. We talked a little more, but, still, my feelings didn't change. I still didn't really want to see her or talk to her too much.

In the meantime, I was getting pressure from my husband and my family to make up. This really, really upset me. It was as if they were all blaming me for the rift, and making my mother the victim. I never ever stopped any of my family to have contact with her. I just didn't want any contact myself.

"It was really hurtful to hear that my own children thought about it that way. They treated me as if I were the bad one, as if I were an awful person because I wasn't able to forgive my mother for all the pain she had caused me. I was in a lot of emotional pain. Now, even my children made me feel that I was doing something wrong. What did I do to deserve that?

"I understand now that they felt like they were stuck in the middle. My mother would ask them why I didn't want any contact with her, and she kept on harassing my daughters about it. That must have been hard on them, and I never intended to put them into that position. I'm sorry that they had to deal with that.

"I guess it shows again how insensitive my mother is, not being able to realize that it doesn't have anything to do with my daughters. Again, she tried to manipulate other people to get to me.

"Then, some months after that, I thought, *How come I can't forgive her? I'm a good person. Shouldn't I be able to forgive her? Shouldn't I find it in my heart to forgive her? Isn't that what good people are able to do?*

"It wasn't like I didn't want to forgive her. I just had no idea how to do that. I had forgiven many people in my life who had deeply hurt me. What they did to me no longer hurt, and it was easy to forgive them. So why couldn't I forgive my mother? Was it because it was still hurting so much? "Those were the thoughts going around in my mind for some time. I wanted to forgive her, but I didn't know how. I was still hurt. I was no longer angry, but I was still very much hurt.

"Then one day, I found myself talking to the universe (some would call this praying). I told the universe that I really wanted to be able to forgive my mother, but that I had no idea how to do that. I must have said something like, 'I really want to forgive my mother for all those times that she deeply hurt me, but I don't know how. Can you please help me to have it in my heart to forgive her?' And then I let it go. I didn't even think about it anymore for several months.

"Then in March, I got engaged and, as I was planning my wedding, I was inclined to call my mother to tell her about my engagement and to invite her to my wedding. So I did.

"Had I totally forgiven her at the time? No, I hadn't, but I think I had opened up my heart for the possibility of forgiveness. Again, I didn't give it any thought at all. I just called my mother without even thinking of it.

"Then at my wedding, we spent an amazing week with our closest family and friends. It was so beautiful, warm, and loving to have all our dear ones with us. And, yes, my mother was part of it, and I could see that she really enjoyed it.

"Had I totally forgiven her at that time? I don't know, but I felt no more pain, no more distress, or anything like that. I remember my sister asking why I had invited my mother, and I told her that I really didn't know why or what had happened.

"Then about six months after the wedding, I told my husband that I wanted to invite her for the upcoming Christmas and pay for her ticket. She wasn't getting any younger, and, by then, she'd have three great-grandkids living here in Australia while she lived in the Netherlands. I thought that it would be great for her to be there and meet the newest addition to the family, especially as it might well be the last time for her to be able to travel this far.

"That was when I realized that I had truly forgiven her...effortlessly. How? Well, to be honest, I still don't know. The only thing I can think of is that I had some help from the universe. I had forgiven her, and I was fine with her being around. Probably even more, I wanted her to have a great time, to be part of the family here in Australia.

"Talk about miracles; this certainly had been a big one. Going from not wanting to see her and not wanting to talk to her ever again to now even inviting her and paying for her ticket is pretty amazing. And that happened without any effort, without any pain, without even any thought. So really, I cannot even give myself a pat on the back. I truly didn't put any effort into forgiving her. It just happened.

"I've forgiven her, and I think that I've come to accept her even though I may not always like what she's doing. The most amazing thing is that this all happened without any pain, without any effort, and even without thinking about it."

How do you feel now that you have forgiven your mother?

"It's strange, but I feel like a big weight has been lifted from my shoulders. What happened no longer hurts, and I can move on without anger and without regrets."

Do you deserve a pat on your shoulders?

"No. Although it's something I'm very happy about, I cannot pat myself or compliment myself. I almost feel like I haven't really done anything at all. I asked for help to forgive my mother, and I received help. The intention was honest, but I feel that it wasn't me doing the forgiving. It all happened without pain and without any effort. But I can breathe knowing that I didn't leave that relationship in anger and hurt."

Again, what happened was that you created forgiveness by thought, intention, emotion, and action. See, you're able and are doing this more often than you realize and give yourself credit for.

You forgave your mother. Has this also changed the way you see her?

"Yes, I look at her differently now. I realize more and more that we're all on our own journey and that we're all at different levels of understanding and of ability to love.

"It looks like my mother often acts like a five year old who's trying to get her way and being selfish and childish. In a way, I feel sorry for her, that she feels she needs to act like that. I wonder if behaving like that really makes her feel happy. But anyway, she must make her own choices and she's responsible for her own life.

"I've forgiven her and I talk to her again, but that surely doesn't mean that I'm back being that little girl. I have my boundaries, and am a very strong person now. I know who I am, and that certainly isn't who my mother believes I am.

"That's fine. We can just have a more superficial relationship. We can chat about the weather and about her house, her car, her hobbies, and leave it at exactly that. I have no need to have a deep and meaningful relationship with her. She's my mother, and, as such, I have accepted her back into my live. But that's as far as it goes."

Reflection:

- **Forgiving the people who hurt you will set you free**

My Motherhood Joy

***

Tell me about being a mother yourself, how do you see your role?

"The main thing for me as a mother has always been to show them I love them as much as I can. This means saying 'I love you' to them on a regular base. Kids need to know and need to hear that they are loved, even when they make mistakes or do bad things."

"Isn't that difficult to do?

"In general, no, that wasn't too difficult to do. They are kids that need to learn and experience, and I've always strongly felt that, as parents, we're there to guide them. Obviously, they make mistakes, just as we all do. Looking back, I believe I loved and still love them unconditionally. This was easy, as they were pretty good kids. That doesn't mean that I was never angry with them. Of course, at times, I would be upset with them. I think you can say that I could be upset about what they were doing, but I loved them for who they were.

"The other thing that has always been important to me is that I would give them a lot of freedom to go their own way, do their own thing, and be responsible for their own actions, all of course within certain boundaries. At times, I've been afraid that I gave them too much freedom. It's very hard to draw a line there."

So, why did you give them too much freedom? Because you didn't have that when you were young?

"You're right. I probably gave my kids a fair amount of freedom because I felt that, as a child, I didn't have any freedom at all.

"What I've always tried to keep in mind is that they're different to me. They are different human beings with other needs and other dreams and hopes.

"I've tried to support them as much as I could to live their own lives, be who they want to be. By support, I mean giving advice where needed and accepting it when they wouldn't take it on, helping them in every way possible, and being there for them whenever they would fail, or whenever they needed help.

"I wanted to create an environment for them in which there was room for failure as much as for success, I wanted to create a home for them where they could be themselves. I let them know that whatever would happen, whatever mistakes they would make, I would be there for them and I would love them no matter what.

"I wanted to create that safe place where they could grow and experience, knowing that I would always respect them for the choices that they made in their own lives for their own being."

But, how can it be safe and full of freedom? You need to explain that to me.

"It may seem like a contradiction, but if you use your freedom in a responsible way, then that freedom can also be safe. I've been blessed with kids who have a great sense of responsibility. That doesn't mean that they were never naughty or misused their freedom, but that's part of being a child. As a child, you play, push your boundaries, and try new things. That's how you learn. Learning doesn't only come from doing the right things; it also comes from making mistakes.

"I also wanted to create an environment that was fun, and where we could all laugh so hard that tears would roll."

And, have you succeeded doing so?

"I believe in certain ways, I've succeeded, but I also have to admit that I haven't always been able to give them what they wanted or even needed.

But I know, and I think they know too, that I've done the very best I could do, given the circumstances. However, there are things that I would have liked to be different if possible."

Like what?

"Foremost, I would have liked them to grow up with a caring and loving male figure. I think they missed out on having a real dad. As a single mom, unfortunately, I could only take on a part of the male role in a family. Of course, that was never the same as having a man around.

"I regret that my choices of men contributed in them having a less positive picture of men in general."

Why do they need a positive picture of men? They can see for themselves when they are older.

"They sure can see when they are older. The point here is that they had a less positive or maybe even a negative idea of men because of the choices I made. That picture is not a realistic one. I didn't want them to think that all men are bad, as that's not true. There are a lot of great men out there; I just hadn't found the right one.

"I've always tried to explain to them that I made the wrong choices when it came to men and that there are definitely good men out there. I just didn't find one for a long time. Now, I'm in a great relationship with a really good man, and my daughters can see how happy I am with him.

"The other thing I regret is that there were times when there wasn't enough money. My girls have missed out on things in their lives because of that. At times, there wasn't enough money for new clothes, shoes, or even a school field trip. Sometimes, there actually wasn't enough money for food. I know that not having enough money was caused by situations that were out of my control and I know that I did the very best I could. It's just that I know that me doing the very best possible wasn't always enough and my kids have suffered because of that."

Do your kids see this the same way? Maybe you just think it was bad, but they didn't really suffer. Or maybe they understood and respected your choices?

"Hmmm, I always thought that my kids suffered because of the lack of money, but maybe you're right; they might have experienced that time in a totally different way. We never really talked about it, so I can't truly say how they felt. It might not have been a big deal for them.

"It reminds me of something from my childhood. My parents didn't have a lot of money, but when I was in high school, there always was enough for food, clothes, and even a holiday each year. I never, ever felt that I was lacking in anything, but a friend from high school later told me that she felt for me because my parents were really poor. I guess she saw it that way because she had a different point of view; her parents were fairly rich. For me, the fact that my parents were not that rich never bothered me at all because I felt that there always was enough.

"What I also regret is that they witnessed the pain I went through. Kids should be free of worries, but I know that they've been worried about me. A lot of the misfortunes, pain, and betrayal I've been through in my life, of course, have also been a part of their lives. I'm their mom and all I can say is that my wellbeing has an impact on their lives too, as much as their wellbeing has an impact on my life.

"I believe as a mom, I haven't done too badly."

Oh, now you change your tune. I'm happy, but why did you run yourself down all the time to now say it was better than you thought?

"No, I haven't really changed my tune. I think I wasn't a bad mum at all. I probably was a pretty good mum. What I'm saying is that, although I believe I was a good mum, the choices I made in my life, and the experiences I went through, weren't always necessarily good for my kids.

"My girls are adults now. They're strong, successful, loving, and caring young women. I'm not just proud of them, I don't just love them, but I also have a deep respect for them, for who they are now as persons, as women."

Isn't that maybe just because of what they went through?

"No, I don't think my kids are great women because of what they went through. It may have been a contributing factor, but I believe that they're great people by themselves."

You're right. As I explained before, they entered this life with a plan. We enter this life with a character that has been built during our past lifetimes. You can say that your daughters entered this life with good character, and, in this life, they've had experiences that were good and bad, that added to their character and were parts of their plans. So you can say it's a combination of who they already were and of how their experiences in this life may have changed them, or maybe I should say of how their experiences in this life have built on their character.

"Yes, that is exactly what I mean to say. I believe that with me, they both have been through a lot. But, in the end, it looks like it has only made them stronger and it has built (on) their character, their being."

I know that you've always had the intention—and I mean even long before you even had the conscious desire to become a mother yourself—to be a better mother than your mother was. You had the intention to lead motherhood in your family in an upwards spiral.

"I hope I've learned enough from my mother's mistakes. I've certainly tried to raise my children in a different manner, in a more human, respectful way. In that sense, the circle of abuse on the female side of our family has finally been broken. There's a certain sense of pride and happiness coming from the realization that I've been able to achieve that."

And do your kids know that? Do they know your fear and also your happiness of achievement?

"I'm not sure. They know that I didn't have a great childhood, but they don't know about the earlier generations. I've told them that I think they're great mothers, but I've never told them why that's so important to me.

"One of the things that I realize is that my mother has done much better than her own mother. I truly believe that I've done better than my mother, and I can already see that my daughters are better mothers than I've been, even if it was just for the fact that they can spend more quality time with their kids than I've ever been able to."

So, it's slowly but steadily getting better all the time?

"Yes, I guess what I want to say is that I believe that the next generations of mothers in our family have learned from the mistakes their mothers made. I see that as a very positive thing. I look at my daughters, and see the great loving and kind mothers that they are, and it absolutely melts my heart.

"I love being with them and talking to them. Being with them makes me feel loved too. I know they love me and care for me and I know the three of us really make a strong team. I know that when it comes to it, we'll always take care of each other. And now that I have a loving man in my life, it's even better. He's the most caring and generous man I've ever met. And I'm very happy that my daughters can see and experience that too.

"I think that we're pretty close together. I wonder if that's partly because we've been through a lot, just the three of us here in Australia for many years."

You use the term I think *a lot. Now, I think you should make up your mind.*

"Okay, you're right; If there's one thing that's really good in my life it's my relationship with my daughters and husband. Thinking (haha, yes, I do use the word a lot...) of them always makes me smile and gives me that very warm comforting feeling inside.

"I hope with all my heart that they may find in their lives all that they are looking for. I hope they can realize all their dreams and I also hope that now that they both are mothers themselves, they can learn from the mistakes I've made and become a better mother than I've been. I hope they can take all the good things from their childhood and pass it on to their children and do better in all the things where I've failed."

They might need to hear this once more – or twice. Your hope is good and full of love. Help them to make your hope reality. Seeing this will make not only you happy but also them.

"Thanks, that's nice of you to say. I'll tell them in person once more – or twice, as you say, and they can also read it in this book."

"My daughters have also provided me with plenty of good laughs."

Yes, kids will always provide you with good laughs and funny situations.

"I remember that time after my divorce. We were in the car going to see some friends, and I needed to fill up. When I came back from paying for the fuel, I saw my girls, who were about seven and five years old at the time, hanging out of the window of the car, talking to a man at one of the other pumps. They were yelling, 'Are you in love with my mommy? Are you going to marry her?' That was kind of embarrassing and funny at the same time. They were always trying to match me with a new man. They were also asking random men on the street or in a restaurant if they were going to be their new daddy. Well, what can I say? Who needs a dating site when you have kids like that?"

Why were they so keen to match you up with somebody? Did they see your desire to be together with another man?

"I wasn't ready for another man in my life at that time, but they probably thought that, in a family, there must be a man as well.

"When they were just a bit older, I also remember going to a shopping center. It was freezing outside, so we were happy to be inside. We were sitting down for a coffee and hot chocolate. When the girls finished their drinks, they were going to the play area, which was visible from where I sat. There also was a fountain. I must have looked away for a second, because when I looked up again, I saw them with their arms in the fountain picking up the coins that people had been throwing in. The arms of their winter coats were dripping wet. They were laughing and very excited. 'Look mommy, we're rich.' They were showing me all the coins they picked out of the fountain. I wasn't impressed. Obviously, in all their excitement, they didn't realize that it was freezing cold outside and that we would have to walk back to the car.

"Trying to teach them some basic care for the environment at a young age, I taught them not to throw any rubbish on the ground. My younger daughter took that to the extremes. At the age of two, she would get upset with other people leaving their stuff, and she would tell them off in a very loud and angry voice. Wherever we would go, she would pick up all papers, bottles and other things and throw it in a bin. Often, she wouldn't want to leave until all was cleaned up."

Isn't this all showing you that they followed you whatever you did? You gave them what you could give them. It often doesn't matter what it means to you, but what it means to them.

"Like you say, kids interpret things in their own way and they give their own meaning to it. In this case, I showed them not to throw any rubbish on the ground, and my younger daughter understood that as a guideline for herself and for other people. She was literally cleaning up the mistakes of others.

"Holidays always were fun as well, or at the very least, interesting. When driving we would always listen to music and sing along. We all love to sing."

A lot of families can't afford going on holidays. Other families can afford holidays, but don't enjoy them. I think you were very lucky to be neither of these.

"I'm very grateful for all the holidays we were able to afford. To me they were all very special times when we could have fun and enjoy each other's company. It's more than some other families get. Like you said, there are other families who can't afford holidays or who don't enjoy spending time together that way. But I truly loved going on trips with the girls.

"I remember driving through Paris when they were about eight and six years old. There was this one cassette tape that they wanted to hear repeatedly, and they got upset when I turned it off so I could concentrate trying to find my way in Paris. I'll never forget because it wasn't just the music but also the smell of vomit. My younger one was carsick and had been throwing up. She still talks about the plastic bag that I gave her to vomit in, because it smelled like salami sandwiches. That made her even sicker.

"Another time, much later, we went on a holiday in Australia. They both took a friend along each. It was a very hot day while we were driving to our destination, and as my old car didn't have any working air conditioning, we had the windows wide open. I'll never forget the heat, the wind in my hair, and four teenage girls banging their heads on the beat of hard rock music. We had decided that we all could listen to our favorite music for half an hour in a row. Never could I have imagined that all four girls wanted to listen to the same music. So, for two hours, we would listen to their music and then I could listen to my music for half an hour. I hated their hard rock music, but it was great seeing the girls so happy. Today, whenever I drive that same road, that memory comes back, and I can't help smiling. It still makes me happy seeing those girls so happy."

I can see you even smiling now. This is really important to you I think. So, I'm now going to give you some time to just talk about this. I'll be patient and listen without interrupting you.

"We also went to Ibiza on a holiday. It was nice, sunny, and warm, and we all had a great time. A funny thing was that when boarding the plane, the song 'I'm going to Ibiza' was blasting through the loudspeakers. My girls got very excited; at that time, it was one of their favorite songs and proof that they were on the right plane!

"Our holiday to Turkey was memorable, because we had rented a small apartment that was infested with little bugs. It was so dirty. My daughters didn't seem to care. They just enjoyed the sun, the swimming pool, and the attention they would get from the Turkish boys. The girls were about nine and eleven years old at the time, but looked a lot older. They were also very blonde, which was certainly attractive.

"Then we were caught up in an earthquake. It happened on the day we were supposed to fly back home to the Netherlands. For a moment, it looked like we were unable to fly, but then we got the green light. My daughters thought it was all very exciting; the ground was shaking and trembling. That was something different.

"Another memorable holiday was the one in Spain. It was a late autumn holiday to catch some sun before winter would set in. Although the sea was already too cold to swim in, the hotel had a nice pool. Swimming was one of the activities that we all enjoyed, so a nice pool was pretty important to us. On the third day, while we were at the hotel pool, the girls disappeared. They had decided to try out the gym. And then I saw my younger daughter coming back and walking toward me, her legs dripping with blood. What had happened? The treadmill had been going too fast for her, and while she was trying to hold on, her legs were scraping over the belt.

"Her legs were open and bleeding. We got a doctor to our hotel room to check on her, but there wasn't too much that the doctor could do. For the first three days and nights, I sat with my daughter at her bed. She couldn't walk, couldn't sleep, and was in a lot of pain. Later that week, she was getting a bit better, and as the pool was out of the question now, we rented a car to be able to go out and see the surroundings instead.

"My daughter still remembers her socks. On the way back home, I made her wear socks as it was getting colder outside. But then, when we arrived home the socks were stuck on her ankles. The dried up blood had acted as glue, and there was no way to get her socks off without ripping her wounds all open again.

"Over the next days, we peeled off her socks little by little by soaking them in water. I know that it was extremely painful, but it was the only way we could get her socks off. Looking at her legs and ankles now, you can hardly see any scars. Only if you knew where to look, you could vaguely see them.

"On another holiday in France, we were bored. It had been raining for five days, and there wasn't too much to do. That didn't stop my daughters. They found plenty to do like jumping on the bed and breaking it. And then we bought this toy for them. It was a slimy green substance that you could throw on the wall, and that would then make its way down the wall, almost like sliding down. At least that was what the packaging said. Unfortunately, that didn't quite happen, and we ended up with walls full of green snot-like stuff that would not come off. However, that encouraged the idea of driving further down south to find some sun in Italy. The girls loved how I found that place. I simply took a map of Europe, closed my eyes, and pointed with my finger on the map. And that was exactly where we went to a small lake in the north of Italy, not far from the French and Swiss border. My daughters thought that that was really cool.

"One year after we came to Australia, we were on a plane going to Auckland, New Zealand for a short holiday and to pick up or confirm our Australian permanent residency. We could only do that outside of Australia, so going to New Zealand was the most obvious and convenient option.

"My older daughter was sitting next to me in the plane. She said to me, 'Thank you, mom, for this great experience living in Australia. I'm so fortunate also that I've already seen so much of the world. I have friends in my class who've never been out of the city and who've never even been out of the suburb they live in. Most of them can only dream of going overseas and visiting another country. It's also great that I learned another language. What do you think, mom, can we maybe go and live in France next year? I'd like to learn French as well.'

"I found it touching and wise that at the age of twelve, she realized that she had had some great experiences by visiting other countries and by moving to Australia and learning another language. Not many kids that age would have thought too much of that. She obviously had also realized that it was possible to learn a new language in a short time, and that speaking more than one language was a benefit.

"Apart from traveling, going to the beach for a walk was another thing we loved doing. For me, the beach always brings peace and calmness. My older daughter would often come along with me, and we would walk and then sit down to watch the waves, not doing anything really, but just sit there and enjoy the breeze, the sun on our faces, the sound of the ocean. To me it's still one of my favorite ways to unwind.

"My girls were also very attentive. For my 41st birthday, they created a great memory book for me. That really touched my heart, and I often still look at the book and smile. They knew that my 40th birthday had been a disaster. The relationship with my boyfriend was at its end, and he didn't even bother to wish me a happy birthday. I didn't get any presents and, although I had thought we'd go out for dinner, I ended up calling for a pizza myself. I felt ignored, as if I didn't matter.

"So for my next birthday, my daughters made me feel really special. They didn't realize that they always made me feel special, even on my 40th

birthday. The fact that I was sad didn't have anything to do with them. I felt sad about the way my boyfriend acted.

"And then, of course, there were their teenage years. I have to mention that I really liked those years. It felt great having long conversations with them, and it was great seeing them grow into young women. With growing up also came partying and drinking. I remember the first time that my older daughter came back home drunk. She was vomiting in the bathroom, and I was laughing out loud. My other daughter asked me why I was laughing and why I wasn't upset. I explained to her that just the fact that her sister was feeling miserable and throwing up was enough punishment.

"Both my daughters ended up in hospital once because they had been drinking too much. They tried to disguise it. One tried to explain that she had had an allergic reaction to peanuts after going out for dinner with some friends. The other daughter told me that someone had spiked her drink. They had to learn the hard way that drinking too much is certainly not a pleasant experience. In their defense, I have to say that today they hardly drink at all. They're both reasonably health conscious, and drinking alcohol is an exception and kept for special occasions most of the time. I know I drink a lot more than they do.

"Their weddings were special. Obviously, they were special for my girls, but they were also special for me. What else does a mother want for her children other than to be happy? They both looked absolutely stunning and happy. They both married a great guy, and I have a lot of love and respect for both of the men.

"Seeing my daughters on their wedding days was so special. They had grown up, and now they were ready to start their own families.

"To me, their weddings were also almost like an official sharing of responsibility of care. However, I still feel their pains as if they were my own pain. I so do want to protect and save them from pain, hurt, and negative experiences in their lives, but I know that I can't do that. First, I can't protect them from everything. Second, they have to live their own lives and have their own experiences even if they're negative. Third, I can't constantly take on their pain and feel like I have to fix their situations. I have my hands full with my own life. Of course, I'll always be there for them if they need help, and give them a hand or a shoulder to cry one.

"Some of the highlights now are our catch-up dates. We love to catch up over a coffee and have a chat. The grandkids come along and get a chance to play together. It's nice to see how the kids from both my daughters have started to play together. These are the little moments that truly make my life worth living.

"It's also nice to see how my daughters are still teasing me. One Christmas, I forgot to get the turkey out of the freezer in time. That has become the yearly joke. On Christmas Eve or Christmas day, I always get asked if I remembered to defrost the turkey. They make fun of me, but I don't mind. On the contrary, I love it."

Okay, I'm stopping you here for a while. All these are mainly happy memories. I know how much you love them and how happy it makes you spending time with them. But their lives haven't always been so easy and carefree. There was one particular thing that had a huge effect on all three of you. Can you please share that?

"Yes, I'll share that. I've asked my younger daughter for permission to share that here, without going into too much detail.

"During the time when I just started driving a taxi, I noticed that something wasn't quite right with my younger daughter. She was 15 years old at the time, became very withdrawn, and started to lose weight. I tried to talk to her several times, but, for a long time, she didn't open up. Then, one day, I sat down with her to really get to the bottom of it.

"I remember her being really upset. She said that something was happening to one of her best friends, but that she had promised not to tell anyone. She felt that she couldn't talk about it because it would mean that she would break her promise. This I could understand, but I told her that keeping a promise shouldn't impact her life in a negative way, and it shouldn't make her sick.

"When she finally started talking, she explained that her friend was sexually abused by her father and that her father would also invite other men in the house to have sex with his daughter.

"We talked about what we could do to make this stop, and I decided to call the school counsellor. I had known the school counsellor for a while, as she was also the mother of a friend of my two girls, and she would probably know better whom to contact. When I called her, she had just found out herself. Then the police were contacted."

But that wasn't the end of it, was it?

"No, that wasn't the end of it at all. In certain ways, it looked like this was just the beginning. The next morning, the father of this friend was found dead. He had committed suicide."

It had a massive impact on your daughter, and, therefore, on your entire family. Can you tell me about that?

"My daughter felt that she was responsible for the death of her friend's father, as she had broken her promise when she talked about what was going on with her friend, which caused the police to get involved. She became even more withdrawn and really started to lose a lot of weight. She became very depressed, and was close to being hospitalized.

"I was very worried about her. But I remember one day, when we were talking and crying together, she told me that no matter what, she was going to get through this. I believed her. At that point, at that very moment, I just knew that she would pull through. It was strange because she was probably at her lowest point, but I had absolute faith that she would get through. And she did get through. She battled and conquered her depression and anorexia. Today, she's a very strong young woman."

This still isn't really the end of the story though is it? What happened with her friend?

"One day, we found her friend sleeping in front of our front door. Her mother had kicked her out and blamed her for her father's suicide. As she didn't have any other family in anywhere close, she didn't know where to go."

And you took her in...

"And I took her in. I should say we took her in. Although I thought about taking her in, I didn't really want to bring it up, given that my younger daughter was fighting her depression and anorexia, and given that my financial situation wasn't good at all. But more than that, I didn't want to put any additional pressure on my daughters."

But?

"But then my older daughter suggested that we should take care of her. After discussing it with both my daughters, we decided that taking her in was the best thing we could do."

That was very hard wasn't it? You now had two teenagers at home with mental as well as physical issues.

"Both girls ended up in the hospital several times. It was extremely hard emotionally, but it was also difficult financially. It was hard to see them suffer so much. My daughter had severe panic attacks, and I remember sitting in the hospital for hours and hours. Her panic attacks would last up to eight hours at the time, and she was hyperventilating so hard and for such a long time that I felt that she might die.

"I remember looking at the clock and see each second pass and feeling so scared and grateful at the same time for every second she was still alive. Thankfully, she made it. She got through every time again."

How did you manage having three teenagers to look after and work at the same time?

"It was very hard. I needed to take care of the girls and be there for them, especially when they ended up in the hospital, but I also needed to make enough money to live. Fortunately, at that time, I was driving a taxi, so I was basically my own boss and could take time off any moment I wanted to.

"Financially, it was very hard, because every time any of the two girls was taken to hospital, the ambulance needed to be paid. I had to take time off my taxi driving and didn't make any money, and I didn't receive any financial help in caring for her friend.

"And my older daughter, well, she was just in the middle of all of this. I know she always acted strong but this obviously impacted her as well. She saw how much her little sister was suffering. She saw how I was struggling not just with trying to stay strong for my other daughter and her friend, but also struggling to ensure that there was enough to eat for all the three girls.

"She probably also felt pretty helpless at the time. But what she most likely never realized was that by being stable and strong, she helped me tremendously. I didn't really need to worry about her, and talking to her was always relaxed, normal."

Coming back to food, this has been such an enormous stress factor for you, so much that this is still affecting you today.

"There was enough to eat for the girls."

But?

"There wasn't always enough for me..."

Let me be clear here. There wasn't enough food for you because you made sure that the girls had enough.

"Yes, I skipped meals because there simply wasn't enough. I didn't have enough money. I did keep a roof over our heads, but it was always a balance of what bills to pay, what not to pay, and how much I could skip meals in order to be able to buy other things that we all really needed. On average, I'd have AUD 25-30 for our weekly grocery shopping. That wasn't enough, and at times, I was really hungry.

"On top of that, the washing machine broke, the dining table chairs broke, and my bed broke. Not having a washing machine was the hardest. Now I had to wash all by hand, in the little time I had between driving a taxi, taking care of the girls, and going to hospital.

"Thankfully, my older daughter talked at school about the situation and they referred me to St. Vinnies. They gave me a bed, chairs, and a washing machine. They also gave me food vouchers. That really helped. I was so happy and grateful for all the help that they provided. I didn't know that I was able to get help that way, and I'm very happy that my daughter made that happen.

"Everything started to change little by little over time. In the end I got a better job, the girls were doing a lot better, and there was enough to eat."

Tell me what happened to your daughter's friend. Obviously, she was having an extremely hard time.

"She stayed with us for about 9 months, and then suddenly, she took off. She accused me of abusing her; she said that my younger daughter was a lesbian and that my older daughter was cutting her own wrists. They were all lies, and it deeply hurt my daughters. It was certainly not nice for my daughters to be accused of things that weren't true.

"To be very honest, for me, it was kind of a relief that she took off. It had been a very hard time, and I just wanted to live my life with my two daughters and get things back to normal. I wasn't mad at her. She was just a hurt little girl, who was going to need a lot of help."

I believe you're in contact with her again.

"Yes, today, we're back in contact, and it looks like she's doing a lot better. We're all doing a lot better. If anything, it has made us stronger. But that time of my life was certainly one of the hardest."

I know that there's something else that you'd like to say about it…

"I do want to say something else about it. Depression still seems to be a thing that you're meant to feel ashamed of. But, to me, it seems that most people go through one or more periods in their lives being depressed. So, it's far more common than most of us may realize.

"Everyone goes through hard times. In this case, my daughter got depressed because of a promise that she made and couldn't keep and because she felt that she was responsible for someone else committing suicide. That's nothing to be ashamed of."

But that's in the past and over, isn't it?

"No, it's not. The thing is that this period of her life is still affecting her in a negative way, even though she's no longer depressed and even though she's one of the strongest persons I know. She's been rejected for life insurance several times, and often has to pay extra for insurance that they allow her to have. It's like every time, it's coming back to bite her. That isn't fair.

"We all go through difficult times in our lives. I have, and both my daughters have been through difficult times. But that certainly doesn't mean that we're weak. My daughters are the most beautiful, strong, independent, loving, and caring women I know. I love them dearly and have an immense respect for both of them."

You're absolutely right. You all are very strong women, and you should all be proud and grateful for the strength that you have within.

Let's talk about something else. You're a grandmother now. They call you Oma. How do you feel about that? You're still reasonably young. Some women would find it embarrassing to be a grandmother because they think it would make them old. What about you?

"Certainly, this isn't a feeling I have. I'm so proud of my grandkids and being a grandmother. Yes, I'm a relatively young grandmother, but I only see that as an advantage; I'll have more time with my grandkids than some other grandparents, and they'll also have the chance to know their grandmother. With a bit of luck, I may even experience being a great-grandmother one day."

Tell me how it feels being a grandmother.

"Being a grandmother is a whole new dimension, a whole new phase in my life. Those little ones are pure pleasure. I'm totally in love with each of them in different ways and for different reasons as they all have their own little (and big) personalities. Looking at them, seeing them grow and develop fills my heart with so much love and joy. I'm so grateful to have this experience and to have them in my life. I'll certainly do my very best to be there for them as much and for as long as I possibly can.

"Sometimes, I really regret that I still have to work. I would love to babysit one day a week and spend more time with them. I often feel like I don't see them enough. After work, I'm just too tired. But they're in my heart and in my thoughts always. I'm a very happy and proud 'oma.'

"I also have to say that I think that both of my daughters are fantastic mothers. The way they take care of their children always gives me a warm feeling. I can see that there's so much love. I can also see that both of my daughters make sacrifices in their own lives in order to take better care of their children. My grandkids have great dads as well. It's nice to see how involved they are in the lives of their kids.

And I have to mention my grandkids other grandparents; they're lucky to have them in their lives as well. Their other grandparents are lovely people and I know that all my grandkids are deeply loved by all of them."

Reflection:

- Every human being, especially kids, need to hear that they are loved.
- Our kids are not our possessions.
- Our kids are their own beings with their own desires, their own paths to walk.
- It's our task as parents to assist our kids on their path without judging, so that they can reach their own destination.
- We all have a different destination (purpose), and will take different routes to get there.
- Depression is nothing to be ashamed of, but please do get appropriate help!

Family Ties

***

You were saying that you regretted that your daughters never really had a father figure in their lives. What about your own father, what kind of person was he?

"To be honest, at times, I was scared of him. I wasn't scared that he would hurt me but just because he could have really bad moods.

"When I was still pretty young, he would kick me when he was mad at me. Until one day, he tried to kick me when I was running up the stairs. My father missed me but, instead, kicked the stairs. It must have really hurt him, because from that time on, he never ever again tried to kick me.

"I loved my dad to pieces, though. My dad was an honest man who would do anything for his family and his friends. He didn't mind having to drive for hours to help out a friend. My dad was the kind of person you could always count on."

So, he was an easy person to be with?

"No, that doesn't mean he was always an easy person. Like I said before, he could be really moody and sometimes he wouldn't talk to me for weeks in a row. That was always really hard. I'd rather have someone shouting at me and being really mad, than having someone who ignores me.

"But he was honest in the way he reacted. If he became angry, I could always be sure he was really angry with me, but I also knew he loved me no matter what.

"I don't have any memories sitting on my mother's lap, but I have many memories sitting on my dad's lap. I think that tells a lot.

"My dad wasn't home a lot. He obviously was working during the day, but I remember he was out at least three nights a week, singing in a choir. I'm not sure if he wasn't home a lot because he was really busy or if he wanted to escape from my mother."

Why do you say this now?

"For a very long time, even after he died, I believed that he and my mother had a pretty good relationship, but now I'm not so sure anymore. I'm not saying they didn't have a good relationship, but I wonder if my dad knew what kind of person my mother really was. I really, really wonder about that. They seemed to love each other very much, but I wonder if my dad ever understood what my mother was doing to me, and, if he did, I don't know if he agreed with it. I don't think that he would have agreed with it.

"On the surface, it seemed that my dad was the dominant person at home, but, more and more, I've started to realize that it was actually my mother who would make all the decisions. If not directly, then she would manipulate or play the victim to get what she wanted. I can see that clearly now."

I know that you have been questioning the relationship of your parents. That started after he passed away, and when you came more into your real being.

"Uh, what do you mean by that?"

What I mean is that once you gained more confidence and became stronger as a person, when you started acting more the way you truly are, you also started having more questions about your childhood. Questioning the relationship between your mother and your dad was part of that.

"What I don't understand is how my dad could love my mother. Didn't he see how she treated me? Didn't he see how manipulative she was? Didn't he see how much she hurt me?"

I don't know if he saw any of it. What I do know is that obviously your dad had a different relationship with your mother than you had. Your dad was able to see the beauty of her soul, even though her behavior was far from perfect.

"I have to admit that you're probably right. My dad must have seen my mother through different eyes. He had a very big heart.

"My dad has been one of the very few people in my life who has always supported me. He would take me in his arms when I had to cry. He would hold me whenever I was sad. That was a big contrast to the reaction of my mother. My mother would say things like get over it or it's your own fault or you're stupid.

"I remember the day that I came home and there was the good news that I had passed my high school exams. I had to cry when I heard the good news. I was just so relieved. It had been so hard for me. After failing the first time, my results didn't get much better and I was very scared that I wouldn't even make it the second time.

"My mother told me to stop crying and acting stupid. My dad, though, understood and put his arms around me. The school system in The Netherlands is different from here in Australia and one of the differences is that you can fail your final exams in high school. Failing means you have to sit for your exams again the year after. If you fail again, then you simply will not get your high school/HCS certificate, which will make it hard to do any other formal education up to the age of 25. After that, you're considered an adult student, and you can study again if you meet certain criteria, depending on what you want to do."

Why was it important to you to pass this exam? Didn't you say that school wasn't really interesting to you?

"It was important for a few reasons. First, there wouldn't be a third chance to sit for the exam until I was 25. Second, in the Netherlands when applying for a job, it does matter what schooling you've finished. On top of that, I'd worked my butt off, so getting that certificate was important to me. It wasn't that I didn't want to get the certificate; the issue was that I was scared to fail and always thinking that I wasn't good enough. School was very stressful for me; therefore, I didn't like it.

"My dad was also the one supporting me going to university. When I started university, I had a disabled husband and a three-month-old daughter at home and I was working a full time job to support my family. My dad was one of the very few who understood why I decided to also go to university and get a degree. He was the one who always was ready to babysit if needed, and he would drag my mother along. He always encouraged me, and he had no doubt at all that I could do it successfully.

"He also had a great sense of humor and would do silly, funny things. I remember the time that we went to Italy on a holiday. At the end of the holiday, the owners of the apartment that we rented put a baby cot outside the door for the new people coming in. My dad jumped in and started to make crying baby noises."

You're now back being your own happy and chatty self. Every time you start talking about positive things, you don't want to stop. Many people only want to talk about negative things. I'm happy that you love to talk about happy events. Continue a bit please.

"He had an outgoing personality and easily made contact with other people. I know that my friends absolutely loved him. He had the art of making every person feel like they mattered. He automatically accepted people for whom they were, up to the time they would do something he didn't like. If he was upset, he was really upset and you'd better get out of his way.

"My dad would always make time for my sister and me. During the Dutch summers, he would come home from work, quickly change, and take us girls out to the swimming pool. He'd take us to our sports activities and really made an effort to spend time with us.

"I remember him driving me to an open day at a university. We attended a trial lecture and he fell asleep. After the lecture, when he woke up he said to me that he could not understand how anyone could stay awake during that boring talk. He told me never to attend university because I felt that I had to, but only to do so or to study what I was really interested in. That was good advice and, at that time, I decided not to pursue any university studies. It was only five years later, when I was truly motivated, that I decided to go back and study to get a degree.

"Although my dad died close to 30 years ago, he's still very much in my heart and still very much a part of my life. I'll always hold him in my heart. My dad was a good man and I love him dearly. I'm always very proud if someone tells me that I'm very much like him. My dad has always been a positive example for me. True, he had things that I really didn't like, but he was a kind and honest man with a real interest in other people. I'm grateful that he was my dad!"

It sounds like you and your dad were pretty close.

"Yes, I think we were. I also believe that I came to know and appreciate him more after his death."

Do you realize that you call your father "dad" and that you call your mother "mother"?

"I never thought about it. I guess that shows how much closer I feel to my dad. I just feel like I had a real connection with my dad. I never had much of a relationship with my mother. My dad knew me. My mother doesn't know or understand me at all."

Yes, that's very clear. You also feel much more connected to your father's side of the family don't you?

"Yes, I do. There's nothing wrong with my mother's side of the family. They're nice people and I do care for them, but I feel deeply connected with my father's family. My daughters, my sister and her children, and my cousins are all clearly part of my dad's part of the family. There's so much of my dad and my grandmother that I see in them.

"I'm not saying that they don't have anything from my mother's side. I can clearly see that we all have our creativity from her. It's just that I see my dad in all of them much more than I see my mother in them."

And what about your sister; what's your relationship with her? You're the older of the two. Do you think that being the older one makes a difference?

"I love my sister as if she were my twin, my best friend, and soul sister at the same time. I think that being the older one did make a difference during my childhood, but now it doesn't any longer. I felt so much love for my sister when she was born. At 3 years and 4 months old, I was older, bigger, smarter, and could do much more.

"I've always felt like I needed to protect her. And I did protect her repeatedly. I often tried to be a buffer between her and my mother. This is probably why now she has a better relationship with my mother than I have. Maybe this is also why my mother has always loved her more then she loved me."

How do you know that she loves your sister more than you?

"Good question. I guess you can say it's more that I feel that. My mother has never said to me that she loves my sister more than she loves me, so I guess it's more a feeling than anything else.

"I was always the black sheep and maybe that's partly because I protected my sister. At times, I took the blame for things my sister had done. Other times, when my mother asked me things about her, I lied to protect her. Sometimes, I pleaded for my sister to be able to do things and sometimes, I simply covered for her when she wanted to go out. I think that's pretty normal. I believe that many older siblings do that for the younger ones. I think that's a natural thing.

"After my father had died, I had an open and honest conversation with my sister about our childhood. Only then did I realized that she also was hurt by our upbringing. Maybe she wasn't hurt in the same way and for the same reasons though. I think that from that moment on we were even closer than we had been before.

"I love my sister very, very much and I know she loves me too. We really know and accept each other for who we truly are. We both know that we've spend many, many lives together. We feel like we're soul sisters, deeply connected beings.

"I had a vision of us living in the 15th or 16th century. We were nuns in that lifetime. We were naughty nuns happy to have some fun with the monks. We also liked to work with herbs and lotions and potions. Then, one day, we had enough of the convent—it just wasn't really for us—and we escaped and lived in a little house on a hill outside of the town. But we were avoided like the plague, and people started to believe we were witches. In the end, we were captured in a witch hunt and burned to death. It's strange how clear my memories of that are."

Hold on for a while – too many new things here for me to understand. Visions, previous lives, joy, and punishment.

May I interpret this for you?

And, what is a vision? You're talking to me right now. Is that a vision as well?

"No, talking to you is not a vision. I'm just typing away here. I didn't ask for you to show up. You just did. As I've explained before, a vision to me is like a dream, with the exception that in a dream, my vision is blurred, while a vision is always crystal clear, and a vision I still remember decades later. Us talking is definitely not a vision. I cannot explain. It's just something that happens when I'm typing. I often don't even think about it."

May I interpret the above vision for you? You had a happy life, but you gave it up as you felt it wasn't the true you. You gave up all of that to be honest with yourself and not only do what you liked but also stop pretending being someone else. Now this came at the price of living as an outcast and finally being burned. Most of society tells you to live your dream, but society also hates people living dreams that are different to their own ones. I know you know that.

"Yes, I do know that. First, it was a vision, and I do truly believe my sister and I lived this life at some time. Second, you're right, I can also interpreted this vision as being related to my actual life now, where I try more and more to have the guts to show my true me, even when people do not like that."

I'm sure you've had other such visions.

"In another vision, we were both in Atlantis. The modern-looking buildings were bright white. We were in a city separated by a large bridge. My sister was at one side of the bridge and I was on the other side of this bridge. I felt concerned. Something wasn't quite right. Then I saw the city on the other side crumble. One by one, the buildings were falling down into ashes. I wanted to go over there to see if I could save my sister, but then I realize that it was all too late. It was too late for me as well. I suddenly knew that we would all die. The city on my side of the bridge would also disappear. For a moment, I panicked, but then I became totally calm. There was nothing more I could do. This was the end, as well as a new beginning."

So you're saying that you lived multiple lives with your sister? How do you know that? Is that again one of those dreams of you?

What does your sister have to say about that?

"My sister acknowledges that. She also has memories of us being nuns in the south of France and living in Atlantis just before Atlantis disappeared.

"We both feel very strongly that we've lived more than 300 lives together. I know; there's no logic, reasoning, or proof. There's just a knowing that cannot be explained."

How do you then distinguish between vision and "real" life? Where are you now? Is this reality around us? For that matter, what is reality then?

"Oh wow, stop there. I thought I was the one with the questions. You're supposed to be the one with all the answers. Good questions, though. I mean, what is reality? To me, reality is what we believe we experience in the here and now. Having said that, I do have to acknowledge that someone else may experience that reality in a completely different way. You may love Brussels sprouts, while I hate them. The other question is, are we truly living this life or is it more like a hologram, a virtual world, from which we wake up one day? I don't know.

"But back to my sister… I know that I can always count on my sister. And I know that when I went through hard times, she equally often was going through hard times in her life. I know she loves me and that she'd do anything possible to be there for me. I also feel that I don't need to hide from her. She knows me, can see through me, and can laugh about my silliness and mistakes.

"I think that what we have in common is this endless zest for life, our rollercoaster life, and the never give up attitude. We're fighters, but in a very human way. We both make mistakes and feel comfortable in sharing that with each other."

But you seem to be the more adventurous one. It was you who left the place you were born and traveled to the other end of the world to live there. What does that tell you?

"It tells me that we obviously aren't the same person; we're different with different likes and dislikes, but, in other ways, we're also very similar.

"We also share the same kind of wicked sense of humor and people always tell us that it's already something to have to deal with just one of us, but having the two of us together is just absolutely crazy. We always have so much fun together as well.

"Thankfully, my daughters also love their auntie very much. They both have a great relationship with her. In the same way, I also consider her kids to be almost my own kids. I love them so much.

When I went back to the Netherlands after I hadn't seen them in 9 years, it became very obvious how strong our bond is. When I opened the door of their house and came in, both my nephew and my niece were sitting on the couch. They were sitting upright, uncomfortable. That changed within five minutes. As soon as we started talking there was this feeling of knowing each other, a family bond that wasn't severed by distance or time.

"Both, my nephew and niece, are very important to me. I'll never forget the day my nephew was born."

Tell me about it. I like you sharing things with me that make you happy.

"Well, this wasn't necessarily a very happy event. A few days before, I was out with some friends, and while I was waiting for my coffee, I decided to call my brother-in-law, as it was his birthday. But there was no way I could reach him. Then I started to call my sister, and she didn't pick up either. I somehow had a bad feeling. I tried calling them again several times over the next two hours, but I couldn't reach them. One of our friends saw how concerned I was. I told him that I certainly was concerned because my sister was pregnant and hadn't been feeling too well.

"He told me that there were two hospitals in the city where my sister lived. He would call one of them and I could call the other one. That's when I found out that she, indeed, was in hospital and that it didn't look too good. The contractions had started at 23½ weeks of pregnancy, which obviously was much too early.

"I raced over to hospital to be with my sister. By the time I got there, it was all going a bit better, so the next day I went back home. Then just a couple of days later, my sister called me and I could hear that she was very upset. The contractions had started again, and it didn't look like they could stop them.

"Again, I raced to the hospital, and when I got there, it was clear that she was in labor. They could no longer stop it. It was another time when I was with someone I loved who was suffering, and I was feeling pretty bad that there wasn't anything I could do except for holding her hand. It was all very stressful for everyone.

"Then my nephew was born. He was so tiny, he could fit in a hand.

It didn't look too good, and the chance of survival wasn't very big.

Strangely enough, the moment I saw him being born, I became totally calm. I had this very strong feeling that he would survive."

How did you know that he would survive? That seems more like a good guess to me than anything else.

"No, it wasn't a good guess. Again, this was something I knew in my gut. There's no explanation for it. I just knew.

"He did survive but had to spend many months in the hospital. Today, he's doing okay. There are still some issues caused by his early birth, but he's in his twenties now. He's the type of person who can connect to anyone, and have the deepest conversations with someone he only just met. He just needs help with certain aspects of his life."

What about your niece?

"My niece was born much too early as well. I think she was born at 28 weeks. She was doing a bit better, but the scary thing with her was that her heart would stop beating on a regular base. They came home with her with a heart monitor. My niece is doing really well today. She's a bright young woman.

"I love both of them dearly, and I'm also very happy that they get along really well with my daughters. My whole family is very special to me."

It sounds to me that you have some really good people in your life.

"I do. My daughters, my sister and her kids, my dad, and now my husband all are positive people in my live. And now I also have a few grandkids. I love them and they love me. And it's often because of them that I'm able to hang in there and keep on going. It's also because of them that I keep hope in finding more people like them.

"It's not that I never found other people like them, but they've been very rare in my life. I'm a blessed person with them in my life!"

You and your sister always get comments that you're so alike.

"We certainly are alike in many aspects, but obviously we're also different in many ways. Apparently, we talk and act the same way. We've had many people commenting on that. We also have pretty much the same voices. When we were young and still living at home, we would swap places on the phone when someone called us. No one ever noticed that we took over each other's phone conversations. We could even fool our mother. Over the phone, my mother would not know whom she was talking to. Funny enough, my older daughter has the same voice as well, and there were times people would mix us up.

"Back in the Netherlands, my sister and I would go away together for a weekend or so, and have a great time together. It was our way to catch up and talk and talk and talk…okay and eat and drink. I miss those times. It's not that easy when you live at the other end of the world. But whenever I see her or talk to her, that connection is instantly there. No ocean would ever be able to break that."

It looks like things have changed during your life. From being very confident and trusting in your early childhood, you went from having very low self-esteem and not trusting anyone, to now having a healthy dose of self-confidence and having some great people in your life that you love and trust.

"Yes, that's right. I sometimes feel alone and feel like no one cares for me. But that's not true. I have at least a handful of people in my life who do love me and who do care about me."

Isn't it a few more than a handful?

"Haha, yes, okay, two handfuls.

"Talking about them now makes me realize how lucky I am having them in my life. Of course, my dad died a long time ago, but, at least, I know that he truly loved me as well. And he's still around to watch over me. I feel very grateful to have all of them in my life."

You sure have every reason to be grateful for having them in your life.

"Yes, you're right, and I certainly am very grateful. They're my drive, and I love them more than I could ever tell them."

Reflection:

- Love doesn't ask for perfection; it only asks for honesty.
- Never do something to live up to someone else's expectations. You only need to live up to your own expectations.
- Sacrifice for the benefit or wellbeing of someone else is called pure love.
- Real love can never be erased by distance or time.

Removing My Handcuffs

*****

There's something you call 'The Handcuffs'. You never say it out loud, but, in your mind, it's there.

"That's true. I don't really want to call it handcuffs, but when I'm honest, I have to admit that they probably were. Removing my handcuffs felt like an escape. I'm talking about my marriage here. I felt tied up in a way, like I was captured in a situation in which I no longer felt free, in which I no longer felt me.

"I met my ex-husband about 2½ months before my 22nd birthday at a friend's party. He had just joined the Dutch army and was in his first 3 months, his probation time. This was something that he had wanted to do for a long time. I guess it suited him well. He was one of those typical army guys: strong, fit, and tough, someone who would fight for his country and die for it if needed.

"I loved the way he made me feel cared for and loved. He would come over in the weekends and leave on Monday early morning to go back to his army base. By that time, I was living by myself and had rented a little apartment. I had moved out of the family home as soon as I possibly could. I couldn't stand living there any longer."

I think you need to step back a bit. It's not clear to me what you mean.

"Okay, let me get a bit further back, so that I can explain. Just bear with me. After my high school exams, I went to an international Hostess school, which I absolutely loved. I did work experience in a hotel in France and wanted to explore the world, travel, and work and live in other countries."

Is that what you mean with escape? Live in other countries and travel?

"No, not really, although that may have been an escape as well. But I mean something else. I'll get to that point.

"After I finished this hostess school, and after I turned twenty, I tried to find a job in the travel industry, but this turned out to be harder than I had imagined, so when a French friend called with a job offer in France, I was very eager to go. I went to Strasbourg and was promised a job in a café.

"The job was there, but the owner was harassing me and making sexual remarks. After 3 days, I had enough of that and told my friend that I couldn't keep on working there. There was no way that I would work with a man who kept on harassing me.

"I decided to go to the train station and catch a train. Not that I knew where I would be heading. I had no idea just yet, but there were several possibilities. Before making a decision, I decided to get a cup of coffee, sit down, and think about my next move.

"I could always go back to work in Switzerland. The owners of the café/restaurant there had already told me to be more than happy to offer me a job. I could also go back to the Netherlands and try to get a job there, or I could just catch a train to anywhere and try to get a job somewhere."

You don't like to plan your life. You just think it's great to do something spontaneously. Are you maybe a bit concerned that if you plan, you might plan the wrong thing and disappoint yourself?

"Hmmm, I never thought about it that way, and, to be honest, I don't think that I'm afraid to plan the wrong thing and/or disappoint myself. I think it's more about wanting to experience a lot of different things. That's very exciting to me. It's like a thrill. Some people may get that from a ride in an amusement park. I get that from experiencing different things.

"Anyway, when I was sitting there, sipping my coffee and thinking about what to do next, the man sitting next to me started talking to me. We talked for a little while and then he asked what languages I could speak.

When I told him I speak Dutch, French, English, some German and a little Spanish, he was very impressed.

"He offered me a job on the spot. I accepted and was then working for him as his personal assistant. He had his own international company that was developing and selling business gifts, so my love for languages came in handy.

"I didn't need a lot of time to think about it. I really didn't want to go back home to my mother, and returning to Switzerland to work there again didn't really appeal to me either. I wanted something new."

You run to new things. Are you running away from something?

"In this case, I did probably run away from something. I was running away from home, my parents' home. The thought of having to go back home didn't make me feel happy, so I said yes, and, for the next 6 months, I was working in Strasbourg. I would handle all communications with his foreign clients and suppliers.

"After six months, however, I found out that he hadn't registered me for any insurance or social security as he should have done. When I confronted him, he fired me and I was left without work.

"I decided to go back to the Netherlands and see from there if I could go and work in the United States. When I got back to The Netherlands, I arranged a job as a nanny in the United States. That would give me the opportunity to improve my English and discover a different country."

Wow, stop right there. What are you saying? You just accepted a job from a man in France whom you'd never met before? That didn't work out the way you expected, and then you decided to go for the next adventure in the USA sight unseen? WHAT? Are you nuts?

"Uh, yes, if you put it that way...."

Running again......

"Yep, running again. At the time, it all seemed pretty normal. I didn't see any harm or danger in working for someone I'd just met. Looking back, it probably was kind of stupid just to go and work for someone I didn't even know.

"It was a really good experience, though, and both my French and my self-confidence improved a lot by doing that. And the job I'd arranged in the USA was through a legal agency, so there wasn't much wrong with that."

Don't you see what you're doing here? Not only are you escaping your home situation. Yes, that's right. But you're also creating a situation that could have put you in danger. It could have been a disaster. It looks to me that you did something on the spur of the moment without really thinking about it. Why?

"I think I needed to be free. I believe that, at home, I felt like a little bird in a cage that looked golden from the outside but that that was fake and too small for me."

We talked about that. Even your vision about your life as a nun is that expression of doing "what I want," and not what others want.

"I think I took risks because I had tasted freedom and I wanted more of it. I also needed to be me, and be able to do what I wanted to do instead of doing what my mother thought best for me."

Did you find out the 'what makes you tick'? After all your adventures, you should have found it. Or are you still searching?

"Well, what made me tick then doesn't necessarily make me tick today. Also, I'm still discovering new aspects of me, so, in that sense, I'm still discovering rather than searching. The big difference is that, at that time, I wasn't happy at all, while today, in general, I'm a very happy person. This means that there's less need for change now. Having said that, I absolutely love to discover new things, and I like a good variety of experiences.

"I know that that the freedom I tasted also came with drinking and sex. I'm not sure if that was because I had the freedom to do that or if it's something all, if not most of the teenagers do. I agree I was a bit of a wild cat then, but not one who was out of control. And I wasn't doing it to rebel. I suppose I did it because I was given the opportunity."

You made this opportunity! Be honest that you wanted to go that way, have these times and adventures.

"Oh yes, I certainly wanted to experience that. Admitting that, I also have to say in my own defense that I was never so drunk that I had to vomit, I never ever have done drugs, and I had safe sex…well, most of the times. It was a new world for me with lots of things to discover. It was exciting, and no one was there to tell me what I could or couldn't do."

I think millions of people go through this, while even more regret never having gone through this freedom to find their own life. You're fortunate.

"Yes, I'm very fortunate. I know this may sound strange, but because of my unhappy childhood, I ventured out and had these amazing experiences.

"Anyway, when I got back to the Netherlands, I'd already planned to leave for the USA a month later. My mother didn't like the idea at all and wanted me to stay in the Netherlands and look for a job there."

Why did your mother want you to stay?

"I'm not sure why she wanted me to stay. Maybe it was because she felt that she couldn't control me when I wasn't there. Or maybe, just maybe, she missed me.

"I compromised. I promised that I would stay if I couldn't find a job within that next month. If not, then I would leave for the USA after all.

"Unfortunately for me, I found two jobs within a week. I wasn't happy about that, but I had made a promise. So I stayed in the Netherlands. If I have any regrets then this is probably the one. I hated being back at home.

"I had tasted freedom, made my own decisions, done my own things, and lived my own life, but now I had to do again what my mother told me to. I had a very hard time trying to adjust to that home situation again. I simply couldn't cope. I felt too restricted, having someone who wanted to arrange my whole life. That's why, six months later, I rented a small place for myself. That's when I felt free again… Not that my mother left me alone. She would still try to arrange my life and give unsolicited opinions about my friends."

It seems to me that you'd gained quite a bit of self-confidence, looking at the decisions you made.

"Well, yes and no. Yes, I gained a bit of confidence, but part of it was also fake confidence. Like the saying, fake it until you make it. Well, I certainly faked my confidence at times. And you know what? It certainly does work.

"I no longer used my shyness and lack of confidence to stop me from what I wanted to do. Many things were scary, but I pushed myself to do it anyway.

"Anyway, let me continue my story… about my then husband to be…

When I met my husband, my mother didn't like it at all. She didn't like him, she didn't like his family, she didn't like what he was doing, and she didn't like what he looked like. There was just not one single thing she liked about him.

"It was the same old thing all over again; too stupid, too poor, no future, not good looking, from a very conservative family, and so on… I stayed with him anyway, much to my mother's frustration."

You stayed with him to rebel.

"No, I didn't stay with him to rebel. I stayed with him because I was in love with him.

"Then, two months after I met my husband I received a phone call. It was a Monday and it was only a few hours after he had left my place. It was the day of my 22nd birthday. At first, I thought it was my grandmother wishing me a happy birthday. But then I understood it was my boyfriend's mother. I could hear that she was very upset.

He had had an accident and was in hospital on the other side of the country. She didn't know where exactly. She had been too upset to understand where he was hospitalized.

"I was in a state of shock. I hardly had any information. His mother had no idea what hospital he was in and didn't know anything else. She didn't know exactly what had happened and she didn't know the severity of his injures.

"So I started calling hospitals anywhere in the south of The Netherlands, anywhere near his military base. And when I finally found him, I learned that he had been severely injured. It would be a wonder if he survived the accident at all.

"I immediately decided to drive down south and see him. When I arrived in the hospital, he was still in surgery, and the long waiting started. While I was waiting, someone from the military came in and told me that they had to fire him. He was only halfway in his first three probation months, and with his injuries, he would never be able to function in the army again if he'd even survive the accident.

"I was amazed at how totally insensitive some people and organizations could be… I would find out many, many times in my life."

How was that for you? How did you feel?

"Well, pretty obviously, I was in shock, almost like I was functioning on autopilot. I made arrangements, called his parents and my parents and his best friend and went to hospital, but it was like my body was moving and doing things, but I wasn't there, like being on autopilot."

Thankfully, he survived, but that certainly wasn't the end of it. The times during his recovery and even after his recovery were pretty hard as well.

"Yes, my boyfriend did survive. He was in coma for a while; they said he was brain damaged. His right eye was so severely damaged that it needed to be removed. His right arm and hand were fractured in multiple places, and it wasn't clear if he'd ever be able to walk again.

"Fortunately, he was physically in very good shape and he not only survived and came out of the coma but was also able to walk again and didn't seem to have any brain damage.

"After 3 months in hospital, he was allowed to go home if he'd take up rehabilitation and if he would have someone at home to take care of him. He had told his doctor that I would take care of him and nurse his wounds. He told them that he'd move in with me.

"I didn't really know what to think when he told me. Was I ready for such a commitment? It was a pretty big step, and, honestly, I wasn't too sure if that was what I wanted at that time. He also had just made that decision without even talking to me."

What are you saying? Did he just decide to move in with you and have you take care of him?

"Yes, pretty much. I felt like it had all been decided for me, and that I didn't really have much of a choice."

No, no, no, you did have a choice, and you made a clear choice for certain reasons. You think you didn't have a choice, because for you the choice you made was the obvious one and, in your eyes, the only one you could make.

"I needed to..."

Hey, do you hear what I'm saying? Do you actually listen to me?

If you do want me to help you, you do have to pay attention to what I'm saying. I said that you did have a choice.

"I suppose you're right. I did have a choice, but felt strongly that there was only one decision I could make. So it didn't feel much like a choice at all. But yes, you're right. I could have said "no.

"I needed to clean out his eye socket, as one of his eyes was so damaged that they had to remove it. I had to cut off dead skin from his hand and arm where pins where sticking out, and I had to bandage it. It was all a bit scary at first, but it's amazing how fast you adapt and how things become routine. I quickly got used to it.

"To me it was more the part of moving in together that I wasn't completely sure about.

"He explained to me that he didn't want to move back in with his parents because his mother would nurse him and smother him and wouldn't let him do things by himself. He told me that he needed to be able to take care of himself again and that that would never happen if he would move back in with his parents."

Isn't that similar to how you saw your life at this time? Somebody who doesn't want to live with parents in order to get some freedom.

"You're right. I never thought about it that way. But yes, I assume he also wanted to be able to live his own life.

"I understood his desire to not go back and live with his parents. And as his parents also lived about 1½-hour drive away from where I lived, I also understood that if he'd stayed with his parents, I wouldn't see much of him. It could mean that it was less likely our relationship was going to last.

"As I did want our relationship to last, he moved in with me. He was found 100% disabled by the army and he needed a lot of rest to heal as well as practice to improve the movement of his right arm, hand, and leg. Over the first few months, he received an artificial eye and he also learned to walk again. He was actually healing a lot faster than anyone could have expected."

What did you live off? Were you working on top of that?

"Yes, at the time, I had a full time job, and needed to work a lot of overtime. For me, it was a really difficult year. Not only did my boyfriend have an accident but also my loving grandmother died, my mother found a lump in her breast, my father had a nose operation, and then they found cancer in his lungs. For about 9 months, I would drive to a hospital every single day. That was pretty exhausting physically as well as emotionally.

"So, my boyfriend and I decided to make the next year a really good one to make up for that really hard year. We decided to get married."

Tell me honestly why did you get married? All your happiness in life was around spontaneous decisions. That doesn't sound spontaneous at all. Not saying it was wrong, but we need to be open with each other.

"I did truly love him, but, looking back, I guess I also felt responsible for him. Knowing myself, though, I would have never stayed with him out of pity. I sure was happy with him at that time. Around the same time, I also changed jobs and we bought a house."

Stop here for a second. That year of the accident must have been really hard on you. It wasn't just the accident, but a year full of other stressful events. What I miss in your story though is any emotion. You're telling it emotionless. Didn't it have an impact on you? I mean both negative and positive. I don't feel any love or affection or even hatred toward your husband either. You're just giving me facts. Where's the emotion?

"Oh, there was a lot of emotion at that time, like you already said, negative and positive as well. It was a very, very emotional year for me. But now I can look back at that time and it's not emotional for me at all, even though it was at the time. Where can I start to explain?

"I did honestly love my husband very much. He was my hero. I wanted to be with him as much as I could. I also realized that my life wouldn't be as I had expected it to be. I had always thought that I would have a working husband and now I was with someone who couldn't work. This meant that I would have to work alone, that I would have to provide the income now and in the future, even if we were to have children. I would always be the only one getting the money in and making sure our family would be financially secure. I would be the main provider; actually, I'd be the only provider."

You were changing from rebel to follower. Do you see it this way?

"I was changing from a rebel to a provider, certainly not to a follower. I sure saw and felt that I had to be the provider, and that wasn't easy. It needed a change of thinking. I found it a pretty big responsibility. I'd always planned to keep working, but I'd never imagined that I would be the only one working and providing for the financial security of the family. That was a shock, a weight on my shoulders, certainly at the age of twenty-two. But I loved him and I was willing to take that on. He was disabled but if I loved him and wanted to be with him; I would have to put up with the consequences. That thought wasn't a very comforting one. Of course, I would do my very best to make it work, but it would and did certainly put a lot of pressure on me."

I remember the dedication and willingness to make it all happen, but I don't think that at the time you fully realized the consequences. You did put an enormous pressure on yourself, as you would do many times in your life.

"Yes, I did.

"When my grandmother died, I was very upset, but I didn't feel that I could show that. There was still this awkward situation between my mother and my grandmother. I was sad, very sad. I missed my grandmother and I felt guilty that I'd never said I was sorry for the time that I hadn't visited her. Now she was gone forever..."

We talked about this before. Do you still feel guilty?

"No, I don't."

Good. Please remember that you were only a child at the time, and you did what you thought best, which was at the time pleasing your mother. It wasn't your fault, and you didn't really have a choice given that you were so young.

"When my mother found the lump in her breast, it was a sort of wake up call. Other families had been confronted with cancer and now there was this possibility that my mother had cancer. I was upset.

I loved my mother. I still thought that I was stupid and that all that had happened was my fault. It's stressful if someone of your family gets sick, and I was pretty upset. Thankfully, it wasn't cancer.

"The nose operation of my dad wasn't a big deal, but it did mean visiting a loved one in hospital again. Then, later that year, I received the message that my dad was diagnosed with lung cancer. He went to hospital for a routine visit, because of a chronic kidney disease he had. And now he had cancer as well.

"Seeing my dad so ill was the worst thing. He had surgery and thank God, that went very well. But then he got very sick. It turned out he had attracted a chest infection from the surgery. Every couple of hours they had to drain his chest with a big needle. My dad looked very thin and sick and I remember one day when I visited him, I was holding his hands and we were both crying. I thought I would lose him then and there. This was such an incredible sad moment. I still get tears in my eyes thinking of it. My dad, the one I loved so much, was now this tiny sick man in a hospital bed who couldn't even sit up. There and then, I thought he wouldn't make it. But he did. He conquered the cancer and the chest infection, and we were all happy to still have him around.

"So, it was a year full of fear of losing loved ones and actually losing a loved one. It was a year full of pain and sadness."

Did you ever think about yourself during these times? Your dreams, your wishes, or just your need for some love?

"No, I didn't think too much about myself. I was on auto-pilot most of the time, just trying to survive and taking care of others. At the end of that year, I got sick.

"First, I thought I had too much to drink at a party, but I only had four glasses of wine. I kept on vomiting for three weeks. Then I found out that someone had spiked my drink at the party. But honestly, I think it was a combination of the drug and all the stress that needed to come out.

"For 9 months during that year I'd driven to a hospital every single day. At work, it was so busy that I had to work overtime. I was nursing my boyfriend, and I had this constant fear that someone I loved could die. On top of that, I suddenly had the financial responsibility of taking care of someone else."

It's like all the bad things always happen at the same time. Yes, it was a very hard year, but you also didn't make it very easy on yourself. Who said that you needed to go to hospital every single day? Who said that you needed to do overtime at work? Who said that you needed to nurse your boyfriend?

I know what happened wasn't easy, but you have to realize that you're responsible to how you reacted. You took care of everyone else but yourself. I truly hope that by now you've learned that you can only take care of others if you first take care of yourself.

"Yes, you're probably right."

Excuse me?

"Okay you are right. I should have taken better care of myself as well.

I just felt that one thing after the other was happening, and there was nothing else I could do but give emotional and practical support. The best thing I could do was just to go on, take things day by day, and try to deal with everything as well as I possibly could.

"This certainly wasn't the best year. That's why my boyfriend and I made a conscious decision to make the next year a year to celebrate. So the next year we set the intention to do everything possible to make a big positive year. We got married and bought a house in the town where my parents lived, and I got a new job.

"I was happy. I think I could say we were both happy. We were in love, by then my husband was doing a lot better than expected and financially we were okay – not great, but at least okay. I could pay the bills. With my salary, we were able to buy a nice little new house, and I got a better job. We were doing all right."

As a newly married couple, it should be better than "all right." Am I missing something here or are you not completely open?

"I guess I am saying we were doing "all right" only, because there obviously was a lot of pressure on me. I was happy with my husband, but I was also very stressed because of the added financial pressure.

"And then, two years later, another very happy event: our first little daughter was born, just one day after I turned 25. She was beautiful! Wow, and I thought I loved my husband. The love I felt for my daughter was overwhelming. I never thought I could ever love anyone this much!"

But during your pregnancy, you also started to have some concerns…

"Yes, being pregnant also came with a certain fear. The question was; was I going to cope? Not only did I have a disabled husband, not only was I working fulltime, but now I also had a little new human being to care for."

What was your husband doing all the time? You went to work daily and organized your entire life? Any help?

"I don't know what my husband was doing at home. He did love repairing all types of things, so he would collect broken appliances and repair them. We had multiple vacuum cleaners, multiple radios, and other electrical things.

"As for help, no, I didn't receive any help. Now with a little baby coming soon, I felt like I needed to do something. Although we were coping financially, my income wasn't that great and there was no money for any extras or holidays. It was only because I was managing the money very carefully, that we were able to live without getting into debt.

"After thinking about what I could do for several weeks, I decided to go back to study. The choice was between Psychology and IT. These were the studies I was most interested in. I was more interested in Psychology, but that was a 6-year study at least. The IT study was only 4 years. In the end, I decided to study Business Information Systems, which is a combination of IT and Economics with an emphasis on business processes."

That was a bachelor's degree. I thought you didn't want to study anymore. What made you change your mind?

"What changed my mind was that I now had a family to take care of. It was no longer just me. Although the thought of having to study was scary, I did want to make that sacrifice for the benefit of my family."

Again, it was your decision to go through this. Not anybody else's. It was one of your best ones, but at a price.

"I certainly paid a price and then the hard work really began. I had a husband and a little baby at home, I had a full-time job, and now also a full time study! Studying meant that I had to make the 104-km trip to university three times a week: 2 days a week from 5-10.30pm and one day a week from 2-7pm. With work, I was able to get one afternoon a week off and work 9 hours the other days to make up for the lost time.

"It was a good arrangement, but it meant that I had a very, very busy schedule. I was making very long days and often I would leave our home around 6am and get back home only after 11.30pm. It all went well, but of course I felt pretty exhausted.

"It wasn't only the working, studying, and taking care of two people at home, but I also had to do most of the housework. All I did was basically work and time for myself was put on hold. The days were absolutely packed, with not even time to sit still and think or reflect."

That doesn't sound like your Swiss or French adventures that you loved so much. How do you feel about this?

"My Swiss or French adventures, as you call them, were just for me, but now my life was no longer just about me. It wasn't even just about my husband and me. Now I was responsible for a little new life. I took that responsibility very seriously. But this responsibility wasn't as easy as my earlier adventures. It was very stressful.

"I didn't complain. This was my choice. No one had asked me to do this. I wanted to create a better future for our family. That meant I had to make sacrifices now. The fact that I felt continuously exhausted was no one's fault but my own. I took full responsibility for my decisions.

"I made the promise to myself to give my studies all that I had. If I wouldn't pass that first year, it would mean that I just wasn't smart enough to do it. If I would pass, I would go on and finish the whole course."

I remember that not too many people supported you during this time.

"Most people thought I was absolutely stupid to even try to study. In their eyes, I should be with my family. What they didn't understand was that caring for my family also meant to me that I had to try to give them the best financial future. I couldn't do that with the job I had. My idea was that I would be able to do that, and get a better job with the proper education.

"I think the only ones who really understood why I was studying, were my dad and my sister. My dad supported me from the first day and, encouraged me. I know he was proud of me and thought I was doing the right thing. My sister never really said anything, but I'm sure she understood. Of course, my husband supported me as well."

I still cannot hear you talking about your husband, the father of your daughter. Where was he all the time?

"My husband was at home."

How did he support you? What did he do other than saying this is great?

"He was taking care of our daughter. Other than that, he did go out to do the groceries, but that was about it.

"I passed that first year at university, with a lot of work and effort but with good results. I had good reason to be proud of myself and to go on and get my degree."

Do you realize that you put enormous pressure on yourself? Do you understand that that was absolutely nuts?

"Yes, I do realize that. I know for sure I did put a lot of pressure on myself. But it was a pressure that was completely my choice. I wanted to study and

I was very motivated to make it a success. I needed to do this for my family, to create a better future for all of us."

Can you see why most of the ones around you didn't understand it at all?

"Well, yes and no. I understand that a lot of people thought it was all a bit too much and that it would be better if I'd spend more time with my family. What they didn't get at all was that I was taking care of my family in all ways I possibly could. I didn't just study and work, I also cared for my family at home. Went swimming with my baby, went for walks, lots of cuddles... As I said, I spent all my time on all and everything but myself.

"Then the second year at university turned out to be another difficult year in my life."

Yes, I know. Again, you did the almost impossible, and again, some people admired you and others thought you were extremely stupid and insensitive.

"I'm fully aware of that, and again I take full responsibility for the choices I made. In this case, too, I believe I did the best I could, given situation.

"At the beginning of the second year of my studies, I got pregnant again. Now I also had to take care of this little baby growing inside of me and take better care of my own body and wellbeing. All not so easy, but I was just very determined to make it all work.

"Then 5 months into my pregnancy, we got the devastating news that my dad's cancer had returned. This time, there was nothing more the doctors could do. He only had a couple of months left."

For human beings death most of the times isn't easy to cope with. One life is going to start while another slowly fades away. How did you feel about that?

"You're not the first one saying that. Several people asked me how I was coping with the knowledge that my dad would die while I was pregnant. For me, they were two complete different things. I never linked the two together. One was very sad and one was very happy.

"Knowing that my dad was going to die was terrible. It didn't really help that my mother didn't want us to talk to him about the fact that he was going to die. She wanted us to keep on giving him hope by keeping the truth from him. I found that very hard to do. I wanted to talk openly and honestly with him, but I was not allowed to do so. The only thing I could do was to visit him in hospital and later at home and put my arms around him. I wished I'd done that a lot more than I did."

And you listened to your mother blindly, without questioning her decision or order?

"No I didn't question her; I was stupid remember? This was my mother's decision, and I'd better listen. At that time, I still thought that I was a nothing, that I didn't have the right to my own opinion."

Strange…you make really big decisions by going back to study, but then as soon as your mother comes in sight, there's that little girl again.

"You're right. I don't think I realized that at the time, but I felt terrorized by my mother. I was scared of her."

"But back to my dad… Because there was nothing more the doctors could do, they let him out of hospital. In the beginning, he was still able to do things, but I could see that his health was deteriorating and he lost a lot of weight.

"One of the things he wanted to keep on doing was babysitting my daughter. My doctor had told me that I could only keep on traveling to the university if someone would drive me. She found it too dangerous to let me go by myself. So the last 5 weeks of my pregnancy, my husband drove me all the times that I needed to attend my lectures and my dad and mother would babysit."

Yes, your father and mother were babysitting so that you could continue studying. Did your mother maybe want you to study even if she never said so?

"I don't know how my mother felt about me studying. She never said anything at all, so she may have thought it was the right thing to do as well, or not…

"Then at the end of year 2 at university, 5 days before the start of the exams, and two days after my 27th birthday another beautiful baby girl was born. There was this new little wonderful human being. What can I say? I was just so, so happy, so in love.

"Giving birth naturally is such a beautiful powerful experience. And then when I was holding my little daughter…well…what can I say? How can you not love a new little life?

"Looking at my dad, I could see that he was very happy too and relieved as well, I think. Then, only a few days later, he was no longer able to get up from his bed. Fortunately, we were able to nurse him at home with family, friends, and neighbors. He didn't have to go to hospital. And then, in the middle of my exam period, my dad peacefully passed away."

How did you feel?

"I was sad, relieved, and proud all at the same time. My loving, caring, wonderful dad had passed on.

"He was buried in the morning a few days later. I was having a hard time seeing his coffin sinking into the earth, realizing that he really wasn't there anymore. I don't think I've ever cried that much in my entire life. That same afternoon I had an exam. For a moment, I doubted if I should really go and sit for my exam, but then I decided to do it anyway."

Okay, stop here for a moment…you sat for an exam on the day of your father's funeral? Isn't that a bit too much? How could you do that and why?

"I know that most people didn't agree with me and were even annoyed and upset with me. But I felt I needed to go. I needed to sit for this exam if only to honor my dad. I went because he had always been so supportive of me doing my studies. And so I went."

Real love isn't selfish, you know. You were right in finishing something your dad wanted you to do. Mourning is not about wearing black clothes and sitting together praising the one that just passed away. Far from that. It's about starting a new life with those who passed away – a life and a love that's not natural, but in spirit and pure. I think you understand that better than a lot of other people. Your dad is living in you because you let him live in you.

"Thank you. It is nice to hear your kind words. It's not often that I get to hear that."

"I remember sitting at my desk just a few minutes before the exam would start, and I was silently crying. I felt tears running down my cheeks. No one saw it and no one knew what had happened. I felt so sad sitting there, with everyone else still at my mother's place and my dad who wasn't with us anymore."

But then something happened...

"Yes, then something happened. It was as if a hand was put on my shoulder and I could swear my dad was there. In a fraction of a second, I went from being teary and upset to being completely calm and at peace.

"I was able to finish and pass all my exams that year with even pretty good results. I'd like to think that my dad had a hand in that. The exam I was sitting for at the time was Operational Research, which is a pretty hard subject for which I hadn't been able to study. Yet, I did pass this subject by exactly the points that were required to pass. To me, that really felt like heavenly invention of some kind.

"I understand that some people were upset with me sitting for that exam on the day of his funeral, but they didn't know how supportive my dad had been about me going to get a degree. I went to honor him and his support, not to dishonor him. I'm okay with people not agreeing with this, but I did what I felt I had to do, and I have no regrets for making that decision. My dad is still very much in my heart, and, since his passing over, a few things have happened that has only deepened my relationship with him."

Let me just take a step back and make this very clear; you give birth to your daughter five days before the beginning of your exams. And then in the middle of the 3-week period of exams, your dad passed away, and you went to sit for an exam on the day of his funeral? That's really full on and a very emotional time. How did you get through it?

"I don't know. I just wanted to make it all work. I was kind of on autopilot, and I believe the delayed reaction to all this came months later."

I know that that has been an extremely difficult time for you and I know that you and your dad were very close and have even grown closer after his death.

You've also learned a lot from that time. His death has given you something really special. It has taken away your fear of death. We'll talk about that a little bit later. It's something I really want to talk to you about, but, at this moment, I want you to tell me more about your marriage.

"Three years after my dad's death, I finished my studies and I got my degree. I had decided to spread the last year out over two calendar years so I could take it a bit easier and spend more time with my family. By that time, I had been able to get a better paying job, so the pressure was a bit less to get the degree in the shortest possible time."

Spending more time at home with your husband was a bit of a shock wasn't it?

"It was a bit of a shock because it was only then that I realized that my husband was able to do a lot more than he pretended to be able to do. He would go hiking with his friends, but, to me, he always said that his leg still hurt and that he couldn't walk for long or put too much pressure on his leg.

"He also said that he had a hard time concentrating, but he entered shooting competitions with his air gun and was really good. At home, he wasn't doing a lot, and I always ended up doing most of the cleaning and cooking.

"More and more, I couldn't get rid of the feeling that he was just faking it. Maybe not completely—he truly had been badly injured—but he was able to do a lot more then he actually did. More and more, I realized that the man I had loved and married wasn't there anymore."

How did you feel about this?

"I felt used; I felt unhappy and concerned. I don't know if he had changed or if I had changed, or maybe we both had changed, but our relationship wasn't the same anymore. Bit by bit, I was losing my respect for him. He was just a loser, sitting on the sofa, watching TV and drinking beer. Often, he couldn't even be bothered to look after our daughters.

"I don't know how long that had been going on. I hadn't spent a lot of time at home and when I was at home, I needed to study and take care of my daughters. Had I married a man whom I didn't know or had one of us or both of us changed?"

Don't we all change – continuously? It's an easy excuse to say people change. A marriage is about changing together. Every good marriage is about finding new things, but we need to do it together. Dream together, and live the dreams together. It's important to have common dreams!

"Yes, I totally agree. The thing is that I was so busy with my own life, my studies, my work and the girls, that often I didn't really think about how it all was for him. In that way I was selfish too. I can only see now that I have neglected him and focused more on my girls, my studies and work.

"I also have to admit that I had changed. I'd become a lot stronger, more self-confident. I'd educated myself, done things with my life, and had read many self-help and personal growth books. It was as though his life had been standing still after the accident or maybe even had gone backward. I'm not sure."

Wouldn't you say that your expectations of life in general and of relationships had changed as well?

"Yes, definitively. As I said, I became more educated and confident. I think my outlook on life had changed."

I remember you described your husband using a lot of terms relating to his physical appearance. Can you let me know which other qualities you liked?

"He was a calm, kind man... I just realize that that's the only thing I can say about him. I truly don't know what else to say. Looking back, I may not have really known the real him at all."

Now you were in a situation where your mental life had changed drastically while your husband was where he was. Or even further back as you said. That doesn't work. Remember what I just said about common dreams?

"Yes, you're right. We didn't have any common dreams. I was unhappy with him now and I tried to find a solution. I didn't just want to give up, even though I couldn't see us getting back into a good and loving relationship. We went into relationship therapy. I really hoped it would change things between us, but very quickly, it became clear to me that I didn't want to go on with him.

"He acted like a lazy, selfish man and I didn't want to have to spend the rest of my life with him. I'd also suspected for some time that he was fit enough to get a job but just didn't want to work. I suppose it was easy for him to have a wife who worked and provided for the family. We weren't rich, but we were living a reasonably good life. I earned enough to keep us out of debt, to pay for the mortgage and even to go on a holiday once a year."

So, all was great – was it?

"No, all was not great, but maybe it was 'great' enough for him.

On the other hand, I was sick of having to care for a man who didn't contribute anything to the marriage himself. There was no more love, no more connection. There was just nothing left."

Or maybe the woman you once were wasn't there anymore?

"Yes, you're right. I was no longer the same person as the one I was before we got married and before I started my studies and became a mother.

"Around the time of our divorce, he needed a new physical examination to determine his percentage of disability. I don't know who initiated it, but I believe it came from the Army, who still paid a few dollars pension.

"Only then did it become clear that he was very well able to work and was considered 100% fit for the work force. I'd already suspected it, but now there was even proof. All these years I'd been working so hard and he had used me. He had enjoyed a long, long holiday."

How do you feel about that now? Does it make you angry, are you hurt?

"At the time, I guess I felt stupid that I let it drag on for so long while we had nothing more in common. I felt used and betrayed not only because he refused to work but also because after our divorce, by some miracle, he got a good job, but he refused to pay the appropriate amount in child support. During our divorce, we had settled for a certain amount in child support, which was very low because he had just started working again and didn't earn a lot. But later on he earned good money and he refused to pay more for child support, even though the childcare agency here in Australia told him the exact amount he should pay. Unfortunately, there wasn't much I could do from Australia. But to his defense, over time, he started paying a bit more and he eventually made up for all the times he didn't pay."

"And now he's not paying anymore I assume. Both girls are adults and have their own families.

"That's correct; now he no longer pays."

Maybe he feels guilty. Not an excuse at all for what he did to us, but he's paying a price for his wrongdoing to this current day.

"He sure is paying a price. He didn't get to see his kids grow up. He didn't even come for their weddings. And, he's never met his grandchildren. He may not even realize it, but missing out on that is a huge price to pay.

"During the time of our divorce, I also felt angry, because he hardly did anything for his children. When we divorced, it was arranged that he would have the kids every second weekend and 2 days a fortnight after school. Unfortunately, after 3 weeks, he told me that he had enough. He no longer wanted to take care of the girls on those days, as he thought there wasn't enough free time left for him."

Did he actually spend a lot of time with them before your divorce? I can't remember you saying so.

"During the years he didn't work, he was taking care of the kids at home, while I was working. So you could say that he spent a lot of time with them, or at least he was there.

"He also refused to pay for a baby sitter for these 2 days after school. This put me in an even worse financial situation, but more than that, I was shocked that he hardly wanted any contact with his daughters. I just couldn't understand that he didn't want to see them.

"After our divorce, when we still lived in the Netherlands, the girls would see him maybe once or twice a year. He'd never called and only if they were lucky, he would remember their birthdays. It improved a tiny little bit over the years, but not a lot. He only seems to be interested if he doesn't need to make an effort."

I think you're missing some understanding here. Would you like me to give you some insights?

"Of course, please do so. Remember why we're having this conversation?"

What you're missing is any understanding of how this all was for your husband. He had had a very bad accident, he was badly hurt, and his future was taken away from him. How would you feel if you were told that you could no longer do what you really wanted to do? In his case, it was joining the army.

He was shocked; he had to find a new way of living, a new way of filling his time in his life. Almost everything had been taken away from him. It was actually a wonder that he didn't become depressed. In the beginning, he surely needed your help and assistance; he was relying on you to take care of the financial future as well. In the beginning, he could do nothing else than rely on you to help him. As you did take good care of him, it became a comfortable situation. There was no need for him to stand up and do anything.

I'm not saying you're to blame, but what you have to realize is that, for him, there was no need to make any changes. Changing his situation, for example, by looking for work that he could still do, would have taken him out of his comfort zone. He was simply not strong enough to do that.

"Hmmm, I have to admit, I never looked at it that way. I guess I did understand that it must have been very hard for him after the accident, but I probably never really understood how hard it was. I have to acknowledge that I probably didn't take that enough into consideration. I was so absorbed with my own struggles that I didn't think about his feelings.

"I'm not saying that I agree with what he did or didn't do, but I could have certainly been more sensitive and understanding of his situation. Nevertheless, there were many reasons for filing for a divorce.

"In a way, I'm very glad he's far away. Shortly after the divorce, I found out that he physically abused my younger daughter, and she needed to see a psychologist to work things through. He abused a little innocent girl, his daughter. That hurts. The thought that he hurt my little baby makes me very angry. It also makes me feel bad. I feel bad, that I never noticed and that I hadn't been able to prevent this. I feel guilty that I hadn't been able to protect her.

"What makes me very angry too is that my mother knew about it. She knew but only told me about it when I'd already found out. I strongly feel that she's guilty of abuse too. She may not have acted physically, but she let it happen. To me, that's unforgivable too.

I really can't understand how people can do things like that. My little girl needed protection, not abuse!

"The thought of it still upsets me. And, at times, I feel guilty that I'd never seen it. My daughter was always full of bruises, but she was a bit of a wildcat that would never look out, always bump into things, and always hurt herself. It never occurred to me that part of it was caused by her father's abuse. It certainly was another good reason to be happy that my marriage had ended."

And...?

"And, what?"

And, there's something else you haven't mentioned about your marriage yet.

"You mean the fact that he had sex with one of our best friends?"

Yes, that's what I mean.

"What do you want me to say about it? Honestly, by the time I found out, I really didn't care anymore. It really struck me at the time that I wasn't even upset when I found out. I didn't care at all that he had an affair. I wasn't hurt; I wasn't upset. I was indifferent."

You were already living different lives with different dreams.

"That's true. I guess when I realized he'd had an affair, it became very clear to me that our relationship was over. It was over not just because of the things he had done or didn't do, but also because I no longer cared. The man I once loved so much was no longer there and was no longer in my heart.

"There was nothing left between us. To be honest, I was probably kind of relieved that he had an affair. I believe it gave me another reason to justify to myself that it was okay to divorce him."

And?

"What do you mean?"

There was something else going on that you weren't happy with.

"He was also gambling. I was upset about that. I was working very hard for the money I earned, and he was gambling it away. It just wasn't fair; it wasn't right. I asked him several times to stop gambling, but his excuse was that he always only put in a little money, and that he was always making money out of it. He sometimes showed me the money, but I thought it was wrong. Not that me saying anything about it helped. He just continued."

How did you feel about getting divorced? Did you feel guilty about your divorce?

"Yes, I think a part of me did feel….well, not really guilty I think, more like I'd failed. I'd always thought that my 'yes' at our wedding meant something, that it would last. But I couldn't make it last and I think that that's something I'm sorry about. I know I did the right thing, for me, for my daughters, but I always thought that my promise would stand for something. I failed keeping my promise. Even though I know that I had done and given all I possibly could, it still felt like a failure."

You're pretty hard on yourself. I think what you need to realize is that you did the best that you could do, and he probably did the best he could do. Are you still upset and angry with him?

"No, I'm not. I haven't felt that way in a very long time. However, that doesn't mean that I approve of him having abused my younger daughter. That was wrong, and she didn't deserve that. Not one single child deserves to be abused. But this episode of my life is over. It's done and dusted in every single way."

Reflection:

- **Don't let anyone hold you back from your path; your true desires are worth fighting for.**
- **Find somebody to dream with you**
- **"Fake it until you make it" works like an affirmation.**
- **You always have a choice.**
- **There's nothing wrong with saying "no."**
- **Only take responsibility for your own wrongdoings; you don't need to feel guilty for other people's sins.**
- **Never forget to take great care of yourself.**
- **There are at least two sides to every story.**

The Other Side

***

Earlier on, you said something that I would want to know more about. You said that after your dad died, you had to do an exam the same day that he was buried. You said that while you were sitting at your desk, just about to start your exam, you felt your dad's hand on your shoulder?

"Yes, that's correct."

But he had died?

"Yes. He had died, passed away, or crossed over as some people prefer to call it."

What do you call it?

"I call it anything. It doesn't really matter to me. We all know what we mean. My dad's death was something that was sad, but very special at the same time. The morning of his death, my mother called me and asked if I could come over to sit with him and take care of my father for a few hours. We nursed him at home with our family, friends, and neighbors. My mother and sister had been up most of the night and needed to get some sleep.

"So at 5 am, I went over to my parents' house and sat at the side of my dad's bed. Two hours later one of the neighbors came to sit with me and about an hour after that a nurse arrived to help us wash him.

I remember taking his shirt off. He looked so fragile. I had this strange feeling that something was about to happen. We washed him and I don't know why, but I was looking at the skin near his bellybutton. I could see his heartbeat. It was irregular and sometimes it completely stopped for a few seconds.

"The nurse looked at me. She had seen it too. She said to me, 'You'd better wake up your mother and your sister. I don't think he will make it much longer.' So I woke up my mother and sister and got my dad dressed again. Now and then his heart would stop beating, and then start again, but the periods it stopped beating became longer and longer.

"I was standing on one side of his bed and I had my hands on one of his arms. My mother and sister were on the other side of the bed. My mother was stroking his face and my sister was holding his hand.

"And then his heart stopped. As soon as this happened, a strong feeling of peace came over me. I wasn't scared or upset. I was sad, but this feeling of peace was even stronger than my sadness. My dad had passed away. I could feel him change. I could feel that he was happy, that it was good. It felt good, strangely enough. I was proud of him and I was happy for him. He did it. He knew now what it was like to die and to cross over. I don't know how to say it, but that made me proud of him as well as a bit jealous, because I wanted to know what it was, where I would go, what would happen.

"At that very moment, my dad took away all the fear that I'd ever had about death. It is a normal, inevitable part of life.

I felt my dad's peace. Him dying in front of me was like a present. That's how it felt. There was nothing scary, nothing weird about it. It gave me peace."

Do you believe that death isn't the end?

"I don't just believe that, I feel like I know that death isn't the end."

Sure you do. How?

"After his death, I started having visions, memories of other lives. I've also seen my dad since his death and I've often felt him near. I've received at least one message from him. Let's just say that I've seen things such that I can no longer deny that there's more out there. Of course, I have no idea what's out there, but there's certainly more than we can see, and there's probably even a lot more than we can even start to imagine.

"In the beginning, I had a really hard time believing what I was seeing or feeling. Sometimes, it was even as though I knew things, without knowing where it came from. At first, I was very skeptical. I'm a very analytical person; I look to see proof or evidence, and it really took some time for me to accept that I cannot reason everything, that there are things that I can't explain. Just the idea that I'm talking about this makes me laugh. Good old rational and logical me is telling you she has seen things. What a joke. Yeah…only, it's not a joke."

Do you want to tell me about it? I know you hardly ever talk about it, but maybe you should. Maybe I can answer some of your questions. You're scared to talk about it. That's understandable. Thing is, for you, it's not some kind of fantasy. It's reality. It's a strange reality that you can't explain, but definitely your reality.

"Yeah, I probably should talk about it, although a lot of it is very strange. I wonder sometimes if I'm not making it all up. But you know, I really don't make it up. Even though there are a lot of things I can't explain, that seem to be out of the ordinary, I can't deny it. I can't act as if it isn't happening. I don't know how to explain it, I don't know how or why these things are happening, but they do happen and, on more than a few occasions, it was even confirmed by someone else. It's also as if a part of me accepts it and knows it to be true, but another part of me is always questioning, 'Am I right, did I really see that, did I really feel that, do I really know that?'"

So, are you accepting now that there is more than what you can see? And what does "see" mean in either case?

"Although I still, at times, doubt myself, and often still have the rational part of me trying to explain things that happen, I'm more and more accepting that, at the very least, I have a highly developed intuition, that I should follow more than I sometimes do. There also have been too many things happening that were out of the ordinary, that were later confirmed by someone else."

What do you mean by "confirmed"? You told someone about something you saw or felt and then they said that that was true or correct?

"No, that's not what I mean. There have been other 'sensitive' people who freely talked about something I had experienced without me bringing it up first.

"I suppose the easiest thing to accept as being true, are the things I see. But the things I feel or 'simply' know are much harder to accept. Especially knowing things is very strange. It's like, suddenly, there's this knowledge in my head. I don't know where it came from. There's no reason why I could or should know, but the knowledge is there."

What kind of knowledge are you talking about? Can you give an example?

"On the first day of a training course years ago I was sitting next to a man and I knew he had to do with something really, really old, like history or so. I couldn't tell exactly, but I knew he was involved with something very old. When it was his turn to introduce himself, he told the group that he was working in IT. I was confused. It didn't fit at all. Later on, during the training he told me that he didn't like working in IT at all, that he'd been studying Sanskrit and that he really wanted to work with that old language."

To me, it sounds more like it was a feeling than a knowing. You were pretty close, but you didn't get it exactly right.

"Yes, you're right. I suppose that what I call 'knowing' and what most people would call 'feeling' is hard to tell apart. I don't know. Maybe you're right and it was more a feeling than a knowing."

Back to your dad. Tell me what happened after his death.

"Well, at first, nothing happened at all, but then, about 9 months after his death, my husband and I were in bed sleeping, and I suddenly woke up. The door of the bedroom was open, and, in the doorway, I could see a figure standing in the brightest light I'd ever seen. I was so scared! My heart was beating like crazy. But then I looked more closely and saw it was my dad. He was smiling at me, and I heard him saying, 'Don't worry about me, I'm fine.' And then he disappeared. I think the whole experience only lasted a minute or maybe even less. Had I really seen this, was I dreaming? No! I wasn't dreaming. I was fully awake. By now I wasn't able to go back to sleep. It really looked like it was my dad. Was it all fake or had it been real? At that time, I didn't know. I only knew it was a beautiful moment seeing my beloved dad again and seeing and hearing that he was well.

"Later, when I was reading about these things, I noticed that the words my dad had used, *Don't worry about me, I'm fine,* seemed to be the exact words that other people with the same experience had heard from their loved ones."

So, after his death, you say he put his hand on your shoulder just before your exam and he visited you during your sleep and told you not to worry about him. Were there any other occasions when you thought he was there? To me, it all sounds a bit....well, I'm not sure how to put it....Strange is probably the best word to describe it.

"Strange? Aren't you supposed to explain it all and tell me that I'm not 'seeing things'?"

As I said before, I'm not here to explain life; I'm not here to explain the spiritual and universal laws. I'm only here to help you make sense of the events of your life. But it's you who makes sense out of these things, not me. At times, I challenge you because I want to see how strong you are in what you believe.

"Yes, I do see things, feel things, and know things. It's time for me to stop hiding and to become more confident in talking about these things.

"I often feel him when I'm driving in my car, and when we just came to Australia, I invited him to travel with me and experience what I'm experiencing.

"Yes, you're absolutely right. It's strange for sure. In the beginning, when these kinds of things started to happen, I was pretty confused and even scared at times. I think I've gotten used to inexplicable things now. Although I have to admit that still, sometimes, things happen and the only thing I can think is …wow!"

Would you say you're psychic?

"Psychic? No! I'm definitely not psychic. I can't predict the future or put my hand on someone and know all about that person. I can't make myself feel, see, or know things. It just happens. When it happens, it completely blows my mind, every time.

"I do have to admit that I am very intuitive, and sometimes I do seem to know things about people that they haven't told me. I'm always very careful with that. Again, I doubt myself at one level and am very sure at another level. It's very hard to explain. It's as though I know or feel or see things, but that my logical brain has trouble accepting it to be true. Thing is, that eight out of ten times it turns out to be correct.

"Anyway, to answer your question, no, I'm not psychic. I've been told, though, by several people that I'm very intuitive."

Are you willing to tell me more about these experiences? I know you normally don't talk about them, but if you're honest to yourself you'll have to admit that they're very much part of your life.

"Okay… Not sure where to start… After I'd seen my dad, nothing really happened for some time. I think the first thing that's worth mentioning happened during a hypnotherapy session. When my marriage was starting to fall apart, and I was working long hours, I got very stressed, and someone suggested hypnotherapy to deal with everything that was going on in my life. I didn't know if that would work, but I was willing to give it a try.

"One of the good things I learned as well was to meditate. Meditation has helped me many times, and I believe it even saved my life after I got very sick. I'll talk about that later.

"On two occasions, my hypnotherapist took me back in time.

I don't know if what I found out had actually happening for real."

Oh, really?

"What do you mean 'oh really?'"

I question if you don't know if it had happened for real. I actually think that you do truly believe it did happen for real in another life, but you're too scared to admit that that's what you really believe. I think that you're still afraid about what other people are going to think.

"Oh, really?"

Yes! Again, you're hearing a truth about you that you don't like to hear. If you want to learn from this conversation that we're having, you'll have to deal with the truth, your truth. You'll have to deal with things I point out to you that you don't really want to hear.

I understand. I understand that a part of you wants the truth, your truth to be out in the open and that another part of you is scared to really show yourself. Tell me again, why are we having this conversation?

"Uhm...because there are things from my past that I'm trying to understand and deal with."

And what would you prefer to be out in the open – an unbelievable truth or a believable lie?

"Uh, I would say I'd still go for the unbelievable truth."

Exactly! I know you for always taking the right way over the easy way. That's how you are, that's a part of what makes you you. That requires courage, faith, and believing in yourself. It also requires that you accept that not everyone will accept your truth, for it's pretty unbelievable for a lot of people. Either you accept that and deal with that, or you go back in hiding.

"I don't want to hide anymore. I know what I stand for. I know what I'm saying; here's my truth. Yes, I know that not everyone will agree or can agree. I know that not everyone has had the same experiences as I've had in my life.

"I can only hope they don't have the same experiences as I've had. Not all of them were too great. Although I know that some people have been through a lot more than I have, I don't want other people to have to go through the pain that I've been through.

"Okay, I think I understand what you're saying. I need to tell the unbelievable truth, because that's my truth. That's what makes me, me. And if I want this to be an honest conversation, I need to dare to be me at any time."

You got it! Are you ready to go on? You were telling me about the hypnotherapy session when you went back in time.

"Well, yeah, back in time... I actually mean back to another life.

I had a lot of trouble walking at that time. I wasn't able to walk for much more than a few hundred meters and it was getting worse and worse. Doctors couldn't find anything wrong and when I mentioned it to the therapist and he suggested to go back in time to see if we could find out if there was anything in the past that may play a role.

"While I was under hypnosis, I went back in time to find myself being a young boy of about 5 years old. One moment I was playing outside with a ball and the next moment all was black. I'd had some sort of accident, and the next thing I knew, I was sitting in a wheelchair. I was a young man then. My name was Pieter. I was Dutch, single, about 28 years old and living with my parents. Not that they needed to look after me. I was very independent and a very positive young guy. I was sitting in my wheelchair and was trying to sort of dance to the music while at the same time annoying my mother in the kitchen. I was just having fun.

"Then I was in a hospital bed. My parents were very worried and sitting next to me. I had pneumonia. Next thing I notice was that I was sort of floating near the ceiling of the hospital room, looking down on my body. My parents were crying. I had just died at the age of 30. It was 1941."

And there your memories faded?

"And there and then the therapist took me further back in time. I was living in France now and my name was Jean Jean. My first and last names were the same. I hardly ever went outside. I lived in this small room with only a bed, a table, and a chair. I had two wooden legs. My legs were amputated because of diabetes. Yes, I actually survived the amputations.

"I was a very introverted person, who only had contact with an elderly woman who came to see me every day to bring a piece of white bread and cheese and, sometimes, a bit of milk. I lived in this little French village close to Paris, but I had never been to Paris. The road between the houses in my village was made of cobblestones.

"One day, the old woman didn't come to see me. A little boy came instead, telling me that the woman had died. The boy's mother was willing to give me food, but only if I'd agree to come over to their place for dinner. I thought about it, but I was too shy. I didn't like people. They looked at me and pointed at me. I was a loser.

"But, of course, I got very hungry, and I finally got the courage or desperation to go out and knock on the door of the little boy's family.

I discovered then that they were nice people, and I slowly started to open up a bit and trust some other people.

"Then at the age of 41 in 1872, one evening, when it was dark outside, I fell on the cobblestones and died. I was looking down at my body and saw the little boy crying. It only lasted a few seconds, and then I moved on."

You mean that during the hypnosis, you experienced dying?

"I'm not sure. I had imagined that the dying process is something you really feel. But maybe I'm wrong about that. It's more like one moment I'm alive and the other moment I'm looking down at my dead body. So, I'm dead.

"I'm not sure what happened next. Some people talk about moving toward a light. I didn't see a light, but I know that I wasn't looking down on me for a very long time. I quickly understood and accepted that my body had died, and I moved on. I don't know where I moved on to though."

You're telling me that you're using one body after the next and hop in and out of them?

"Well, it may be a bit blunt to put it that way, but yes, when we die it's only the body that dies, so we hop out of that body. In the next life, we incarnate into a new body, so we hop into a new one.

"What I learned from those two regressions was that in two recent past lives I had trouble walking because I had an issue with my legs. After the hypnotherapy sessions, I was able to walk a lot better than I had done before. I even joined a gym and became a lot more active."

Do you believe this had really happened? Do you believe that you've lived other lives?

"No, I don't just believe so. I feel like I know so."

Oops, that's a bit of a bold statement, especially coming from you.

"Yes, I know. This is one of these things I seem to know without any evidence. But yes, I know I've lived many, many times, hundreds of times."

Hundreds of times?

"Yes."

Please explain.

"I can't explain it. It simply is. I know. I suppose this is the reason why we sometimes meet people that we seem to have known forever."

So, does that mean that you've met some of the people you know now in one of your other lives?

"Yes. On four occasions, I have memories of another life with someone who is or was in my life this time as well. My sister is one of them and then there's a young man in The Netherlands, a Swiss man, and, recently, I met a woman here in Australia.

"With the first three, I have memories of a life and even lives we've shared. With the woman I met here in Australia, it's a bit of a different experience. When I met her, we both felt that we've known each other forever.

"It was such an amazingly beautiful feeling. I felt so connected, so close to her. I don't have memories of another life together, but I know we've been together before and I know that's been in more than one other life. Again, I can't explain, I simply know. Not that it's so simple by the way. Just after I met her, I had a really weird experience."

Weird? Weirder than the other experiences? I got to say.....

"NO! You got to say nothing at all! More than anyone, you know that I'm telling the truth. You know that I'm right and I'm not making this up. Why are you questioning me?"

You know why...

"No."

"Yes you do. I question you because, again, I want to see how strong you are in your own belief. I question you, because I am you and I know you and I know that you often question yourself. But I also know what you know. I just want you to know that.

"Ahh...this is confusing; do you know?"

Haha...yes I know. You're funny.

"And weird you mean."

No, you're not weird. You're you and you have the courage to be you. I admire that. There are not many people who dare to really show themselves.

"Is that a compliment?"

It sure is.

"Thank you!"

You're very welcome. Now, back to what we were talking about.

You were saying that you know you lived other lives with this woman in Australia and that something weird happened.

"Yes, I don't have memories of other lives with her; I merely feel that I know. Except for something that happened... I was sleeping and dreaming but was then woken up by my own voice. I heard myself talking to her in a completely different language, a language that I'd never heard about, a language with a lot of a, d, b and j sounds.

The moment I realized I was talking a completely different language I felt a shock. It was the same kind of shock that I sometimes get just before falling asleep, like missing the last step of a flight of stairs. I was disoriented for a few seconds and then wondered what had happened.

"I'd been woken up by the sound of my own voice talking in a language I'd never heard before! I racked my brain about what language it could be, but it didn't sound like any language I know at all.

"I told the story to one of my daughters. She looked at me and said, 'Mom, you don't recognize the language because it's from another planet. The two of you have known each other from that other planet.'

"My jaw must have dropped because she repeated herself, 'Yes, Mom, that was on a different planet in a different life.' When I asked her how she knew, she replied that she just knew. She was very firm and there was no doubt in her mind.

"Well, what's there to say? Yes, it does run in the family, although both my daughters have different experiences. One daughter had a time as a teenager when she saw dead people who would entertain her.

"My other daughter would go out flying with her dead grandfather.

"My mother has experiences, but doesn't want to talk about it. She's scared. I also know that her grandmother had 'out of the ordinary' experiences. And from my dad's side, I have a cousin who also has experiences like these. So, yes, I suppose it kind of runs in the family."

Tell me about the connection that you have now with the people you believe you shared other lives with.

"I've lived over 300 lives with my sister. We have this incredible strong connection. I think we both feel we're more like twin sisters and best friends. I can tell her everything, anything. I know that whatever happens, she'll always love me, and I'll always love her. I know she accepts me the way I am and she knows I accept her the way she is."

What about the Swiss man?

"I know I've lived at least two lives with him, one on another planet, another life here on earth somewhere in the mountains, probably around the 18th century.

"The Dutch young man had been my son in a different life.

"And the Australian woman, well, according to my daughter, I know her from a life on a different planet. I tend to agree with her. It's something I felt the very first time I saw her. I also know that we've been together in other lives as well."

You're right.

"What? What are you saying? Are you actually confirming this?"

Yes, I am. But I don't need to confirm this. You know. Okay, let's move on. Tell me some other weird stories.

"You seem pretty eager to hear them."

Yes. I know there are more good weird stories to tell.

"They're not weird. Well, at least, they're not weird to me anyway. Although…sometimes they *are* weird, even to me.

"Okay, I'll just tell you about some visions I've had. Around the same time of having the hypnotherapy, I also started to have what I believed were dreams at first. But like I told you earlier, my dreams are always blurry, like seeing without glasses. When I have visions, they're always very clear and I can still remember the details years and years later. So I should say that I was starting to have visions.

I don't know what they mean or why I have them, but I do have them.

"In one vision, I'm in a big building like an airport. I'm sitting down and in the seat next to me is a man. I believe it's my dad, but I'm not sure. We're having tea and he is asking me to move his teacup to his mouth so he can drink. And then I find myself moving his teacup to his lips without me touching it. I move his teacup with my thoughts. I don't know how I'm doing this. I've never done anything like this before.

"Next thing, I'm sitting in a room with my mother and I'm telling her about it. She doesn't believe me and she wants proof. She is asking me to move the matchbox that's on the table. I'm a bit scared. What if I'm not able to move it? She'll just have found another thing to make me feel stupid. But I look at the box with matches and a few seconds later, I see it move. I'm so relieved and a bit surprised at the same time. I really did it. I can really move objects with my thoughts."

So, this was a dream or a vision as you call it. Do you believe you can move objects with your thoughts for real?

"I'm not sure. I've never done it in real live, but I've been told that I can do it. Of course, I've tried, but nothing ever moved. I don't know. It's not something I need to do. In the back of my mind, though, I have the idea that I'll be able to do it in an emergency situation, when it's all or nothing. But that's just a thought. I have no idea if I'd really be able to move things with just my thoughts.

"In another vision, I'm a mother of three little girls. They're 6, 4, and 2 years old and a handful. I feel tired and stressed and I'm not sure if I'm a good mother. I'm in a shopping center staring at this shelf with little sachets. The sachets have names on them and I have to pick one that will be my son. Only, I don't have a choice. I can only pick the one with the name Rolando. I don't really like the name, but this is the one I need to pick.

"The next moment, I'm in a hospital bed giving birth to Rolando. I'm in labor and really feel the pain of contractions; they're coming faster and faster and are stronger and more painful every time. Doctors and nurses are gathered around me and they seem to be very upset. I have no idea why. They're pushing on my tummy and don't understand what happened to the baby. I panic. Where's my baby, where's my Rolando? He's no longer inside of me.

"I look around and see him on a tiny bed with a white sheet over him. Why did they cover him up like that? I take him in my arms and I'm filled with love. He is my little beautiful baby boy. I found him and all my fear and pain disappear. Then I look around me and see myself in the hospital bed surrounded by a lot of hospital staff. I don't care what they think or say. I'm happy, because I found my baby."

What do you think happened here? It sounds almost like both you and the baby died.

"Yes, I believe that's true. I think that at the moment I was looking for Rolando I hadn't realized that I'd died or that he'd died. I think I only had a vague idea of that when I saw all those people around my bed looking at me and pushing on me."

Was it a scary thing?

"No, not at all, it was all pretty normal. Only the feelings of giving birth and the panic of not being able to find my baby at first were really intense. Those feelings and the pain were very real.

"It's amazing, these visions are from around 1995, so it sure is a long time ago, but all the images are still so fresh. It's like it happened yesterday."

And?

"And what?"

There's a bit more to it. Can you tell me about it?

"Yes, okay. I have recently been told that I had a son called Rolando in a past life. During that life, we had a very strong bond, and we promised each other that we would be together again. Apparently, this was around the time of *The Little House on the Prairie*, the TV series, so around 1880-1890. We were farmers. I was married and had Rolando. Then my husband died, and Rolando took over the role of the man in the house and on the farm. Later on, I remarried and had two little girls. My new husband told Rolando that he was free now to live his own life. He was always welcome but he didn't need to feel obligated to stay and help out. Rolando traveled a bit, but then came back to live with us.

"In this current life, I got pregnant with him again, but as my health wasn't too great, he decided that it would be better for him not to be born. I had a miscarriage when I was 6 weeks pregnant. He would have been born exactly two years after my youngest daughter was born. Knowing that he sacrificed his own life to save mine fills me with awe. I'm very grateful for what he did.

"Years later, when my older daughter was a teenager, she told me that he visited her with a message for me. Rolando told her to tell me that he is fine and not to worry. It seems that this was a bit more than just a vision. I really did have a son called Rolando and he is still a big part of my life."

Thank you for sharing that. I know that you have finally found him again, and that you can put your worries to rest now. I know you'll always love him and that he'll always love you too. Even though he's in the spirit world now, you have a really strong connection. You know that he's there not just looking after you but also looking after his two sisters, your daughters in this life.

At the same time of that vision about Ronaldo, I know that you had another vision. Tell me about it.

"I truly don't want to talk about that vision. It's too weird, and the rational side of me tells me that it can't be right."

Yes, your rational side is constantly arguing with you. It's true that some things can be explained on a rational level. And, I know you're a very rational person. That's why you have such issues coming to terms with this, and understanding this.

However, there's nothing to understand. This just happened. You know very well that there are things that you cannot explain, things that you cannot see, and things that logically would not be able to occur.

Yes, this is one of these things. It's a vision you had that's very real to you, even though it doesn't make sense and you can't explain it. Just talk to me about it.

"This vision is weird, strange, however you want to say it, not just because of the vision itself but because, years later, two people actually referred to it as being true. That, on the one hand, reassured me that if I were crazy, at least I wasn't the only one. On the other hand, it also kind of freaked me out."

It sure does. Now, are you ready to talk?

"Well, not really, but I guess you're not going to let it go. You're pretty persistent.

"Okay then, here I go... I'm in a field with green fresh grass. It's early in the morning and the sun is about to rise. When I look up, I see trees and a fence in the distance. Next to me, stands a tall blond woman. She is very lanky. She seems to be very nice, and I feel happy with her next to my side. I like her although I've never met her before. I call her Almira.

"I'm about 5 years old, and I'm a little cold. It's been a fresh night and there are still a few stars in the sky. Then, out of nowhere, a UFO appears and lands on the grass, close to the fence and the trees. Two little men come out the UFO. One seems to be the leader. I don't hear a sound, but he is talking to me, saying, 'You don't remember, but you're not from here. I need you to make a choice right now. Do you want to return where you came from or do you want to stay here?'

"I think for a moment and then tell him that I'll stay here on earth. He's okay with that, and, before I realize it, the UFO has disappeared and it looks like nothing has ever happened."

Yes, that's the vision I was talking about. In my opinion, they're all dreams. Intensive dreams I have to say, but nothing more or less than that.

"Are you challenging me now? First, you're telling me that there are things we can't explain. Now you're questioning me.

"Maybe you're right. I don't know. But there's this nagging feeling that there's more to it. Only I can't put my finger on it. Somehow, it feels important, like it does have some meaning. But I have no idea what it could mean.

"Maybe you're right and they were nothing more than just dreams.

But.... I can't help but thinking this vision was real, especially since two other people made a reference to it. Maybe I'll find out. Maybe I'll never know..."

Do you think it really happened?

"I don't know. For a long time, I thought that they were intensive dreams like you were suggesting, but then I realized that they were more like visions than dreams and, years later, something happened related to the last dream, and I can't help but wonder if maybe, just maybe, there could be some truth in it... That's probably also the reason why I'm telling you about it."

Yes, I know. As you said, something happened years later that relates to it. Are you going to tell me about it?

"No, not now. I'll tell about it later, but, for now, I think I need a bit of a break. This talking to you is all very intense for me."

Okay, I understand, just as long as you don't quit. You have a lot more to talk about and a lot more to tell and to explain.

Reflection:

- Death is only a new beginning.
- With our earthly understanding and consciousness, we cannot reason nor understand all that is.

Surviving The Rollercoaster

***

All right, let's move on. Tell me what happened after your divorce. You met someone...

"Yes, about a year after my divorce I met someone. He was kind and warm, easy to get along with and we seemed to have a lot in common. I really thought we had a good relationship, a connection. But, in the end, it didn't turn out that well. He was just another person taking advantage of me.

"But yeah, in the beginning, it all looked great. We got along really well and my daughters got along well with him too. I have to say that he always was more of a dad to them then their real dad.

As he lived about a 1½-hour drive from my place, he would come over to spend the weekends with me and my daughters. Every weekend we would all do something fun; go for a bush walk, take the girls to a playground, have lunch somewhere, go to the beach. It was always a good time.

"One morning, during the week, when I woke up and opened my curtains, I saw seven round circles on my window. They looked absolutely beautiful. I didn't know how they got there. It tried to see if maybe it was the sunlight causing it to appear, but that didn't seem to be the case. I thought they were on the inside of the window, but when I tried to see if I could get it off, they were still there when I wiped my window with a cloth. I also wiped the outside of the window, but the circles didn't disappear. I was puzzled. I had no idea what they were or what had caused them.

"At night, they seemed to have disappeared, but then the next morning they were there again. For a few weeks, they were there every morning and I couldn't explain it.

"I had my boyfriend have a look at them when he was over during the weekend, but he couldn't make any sense of it either. Then, one morning, I was driving to work and one circle appeared in the mirror of my car. I was really puzzled now. What was it, what did it mean, if it meant anything at all?"

So another "out of the ordinary" thing happening. Don't you think it was just the weather and light that was causing this?

"Yes, at first, that was exactly my thought as well, but weather and light conditions weren't the same every day, and it happened over a period of days. It just couldn't be the weather, light, or something that was on the window. Why would I then see the same of circle in my mirror in the car?

"I talked to a colleague who was into these kinds of things. He couldn't tell me what it was, but he said that he kept on hearing the words "stones and runes." And, I don't know why, but I had to immediately think of Stonehenge in the UK.

"That evening, my boyfriend called. He told me he had had a very interesting day. The day before he'd been thinking to take me for a short trip to the UK, to see Stonehenge. When I heard that, I got goosebumps, but it wasn't all he had to tell. He said, 'You know, I don't have a lot of money, but I went to the travel agency anyway to get some brochures. When I got back home, my father said he had a surprise for me. My grandmother had given him some money and my father wanted me to have some of it to take you for a short trip. He said it would be lovely if I would take you to the UK in spring.'

"Coincidence? I don't know. It would be a bit much to just be a coincidence, I think."

You don't believe in coincidence?

"No, not really. Once I had a vision. I was at a party, some type of official party. Then I saw Einstein. He looked at me and, via telepathy, told me, 'You're absolutely right, coincidence does not exist. Never forget that.' It was great to meet him. He's such a sweet, funny, and very cheeky man. I absolutely love him."

"More and more. I believe things happen for a reason. We meet certain people for a reason; we choose to go one way instead of the other way for a reason. I don't know. Some people say that you already have chosen your path before you were born. They say you've already defined what's going to happen in your life."

I know we already talked about this before. Do you still think they're right?

"I don't know. Sometimes, it seems to make sense. If that's true, then I've chosen the life I'm living now, the path I'm travelling now. It means that I've chosen all the bad, hard, difficult times to be part of my life. It would actually mean that I'm completely responsible for my life, everything that has happened and that still will happen.

"That's not a very nice thing to realize. In that case, I've chosen to go through all the pain and all the hurt. Why would I do that?"

You said before we choose our destination but not the way to get there. Is that still true?

"Yes, that's still true. I know it's true, but I don't always like it, and I often forget about it.

"Knowing myself the way I do, I know I would have chosen the right way over the easy way. I'll always try to choose the right over the easy. Not that I always do that, but I do try. That sometimes means that I get hurt. I realize that. I understand that some of the choices I've made in my life had nothing to do with trying to get the easy way out. I've tried to do what's right in my eyes. I have a strong need to do what mirrors who I believe I am. Even if that means it's a hard thing to do.

"I'm truly trying very hard to live by my standards. I believe I'm a good person, so I have to do good. If I were to do bad things, it wouldn't represent who I believe I am. And it's my choice to live that way. It would have been a lot easier if I chose the easy way, but that isn't what I'm about."

What are you about?

"Like I said, I'm about trying to do what mirrors my belief of who I am, and I'm about love, kindness, acceptance, warmth, courage, inner power, and strength. I'm about being who I really am, as much as I dare to do that.

"More and more, I try to find the courage to show ME instead of a woman people like to see. I'm me, and I couldn't be anyone else. Nobody can be somebody else, at least not for long. I'm about voicing my truth, even though a lot of people may not agree or may think I'm a bit strange at the least."

How does that impact your work life? You can't just say what you think at work. Let me rephrase; you shouldn't say what you think most of the times.

"Well, as you already know, this is a very hard thing for me at work. And I'm not even talking about me telling people of my 'out of the ordinary' experiences. Even just voicing my opinion isn't always appreciated at work. I'll say more about that later.

"I'm about making a difference in other people's lives, although that isn't always easy either. I often feel like there's not enough time in the day to do what I'd really like to do. But I do understand that however little you contribute to the community or to someone else's life, it's still a contribution. Help doesn't always have to come in a big way. Often just a conversation is already helping."

Can you please tell the starfish story? I think that would nicely illustrate how you can already do good by only helping just one person (or animal in this case).

"Yes, that's a great story.

"Two men are walking on the beach, and they see that there are many, many starfish that have been stranded on the sand that will die if they don't get back into the water. One of the men picks up one of the starfish and throws it back into the water.

"The other man says, 'Why are you doing that? There are so many starfish here on the beach. It doesn't make any difference.'

"The first man answers, 'But it does make all the difference to this one starfish that I helped back into the water!'"

Can you please also share the story about the flower that you received? That's such a great example of how one little thing can make such a difference.

"It happened during the time I was driving a taxi. I had finished for the day after a 12-hour shift, and I had left the car where my night driver lived. That meant I had a 20-minute walk back home. I was exhausted and felt really down. Earlier that day, I had left my bag with 400 dollars, my earnings, at a toilet block. When I realized that, I went back, but the bag with money was no longer there. I had lost a lot of money, and that didn't make me happy. So here I was, walking back home feeling tired and sad. Then I saw two high school girls walking towards me. They were carrying a bunch of flowers and were looking at me and laughing. I felt like they were laughing about me, about the uniform I was wearing, or about something else. That made me feel even worse. But then, when I was just a few steps away, one of the girls handed me one of the flowers. The girls smiled at me, and said, "I hope you have a great day." That almost made me cry. That one small gesture, the flower and the friendly words, made my life better. It probably wasn't even a big thing for them, but it made all the difference in my life at that very moment. I often still think about this. I felt so grateful for that nice gesture of these girls. It was exactly what I needed to lift my spirits.

"So even if you only help one person, it may not seem like a lot, but it will certainly make a difference for that particular person. Nevertheless, I've always felt like I could do more to help others.

I guess that having to work and the fact that I'm always tired stands in the way of doing more than I do right now. I often feel that I really don't do anything at all. And..."

Yes?

"Yes, what?"

Yes...what else were you going to say?

"Only that...I just realized that in the past, when I was trying to make a difference in some other people's life, when I tried to help or be there for someone...Well, at times, I suppose I forgot about my own well-being. Almost like I was giving, when there wasn't much left for me to give or when I was in need of some help and love myself.

"It's what I've said before; I've often felt that I've always taken care of other people, but for a very long time, no one took care of me. That hurts, and it means that, at times, I have taken so much care of other people that I didn't take care enough of myself."

You're right in that you need to look after yourself, as, otherwise, you cannot sustain helping others. But...

"But what?"

There are times of only giving and there are times of only receiving. And the ones who receive don't always give back what they received. It's just that all hangs together and while we're individuals, the help you give is for the greater everything and this greater thing will help you. If....

"If what?"

If you accept help. I leave it there for the moment.

"No, no, don't leave it there. I don't fully understand what you were saying before about the greater everything. Can you please explain?"

What I meant with that is that when you provide help, you don't just only help that one person or group of people. What is happening is that your help has a ripple effect. Even when this person you helped isn't passing on the help, the universe has picked it up, and you could say that it's spreading the love.

"Okay, thanks, now I understand.

I think if there's anything big I really need to learn then it's to take care of myself. I always push myself, thinking I can do it all, thinking I can handle anything, thinking I can do it all by myself. But the truth is that I too need a little bit of help now and then. I need a little bit of love and, sometimes, I need someone to take care of me. I find it very hard though to ask for help. To me, it feels like I've failed."

I am happy you now brought it up yourself. Does that mean that if someone needs help, you believe that that person has failed?

"No, not at all. It's just human to need help. You can't do it all by yourself."

Then, why do you feel you've failed when you need help?

"I don't know. It's probably a combination of factors..."

Yes...tell me.

"From what I understand, it's probably a combination of my childhood, when I had to be perfect, and the fact that the few times I asked for help, I got a no as a reply."

You didn't really ask for much help at all in your life. There have only been very few times that you asked for help and that was only when you really, really needed help at the time. That was for example when you were hungry and asked your mother for a little bit of money. You didn't even ask for much. You asked for $100 so that you could buy a pair of shoes for your daughter and so that you would have a bit more to eat.

I believe your problem with asking for help and the need to be perfect comes directly from your childhood. You were never good enough in the eyes of your mother, who made you feel really guilty about a lot of things, even things you had nothing to do with.

"Yes, you're probably right...okay, you are right. But I do want to say that my dad, my sister, my daughters, and now my husband have always been there for me. But during my childhood, I didn't trust anyone, not even my dad and sister. And yes, I do get help from my daughters, but they're my daughters, and I'm their mom. I have to be there for them more than the other way around. I'm still the parent, so, in my eyes, I should be there to help them, instead of them being there to help me. I know that over time, when I get older, that will change, but, at this moment, I need to be there for them and not the other way around. Why else would I be the parent?

"Anyway, I want to move this conversation back to the conversation we had before, to my then boyfriend. We ended up going to the UK during the Easter Weekend and had a great time. We visited several places including Stonehenge and other stone circles. I was a little bit disappointed that nothing remarkable happened.

"Did the circles on my window really have to do with this? I still don't know. It was a bit strange though that the circles had disappeared when we came back from the UK. After that, I never saw those circles again except on photos."

Yes, coming back to that, what do you believe it meant? I know they didn't leave a written message or so, but if you'd have to guess, why do you think they appeared on your window?

"I don't know. A circle has no beginning, nor end, I think it's a beautiful form, and seven circles...well, seven has always been my favorite number. It was almost as though they just wanted to say hello and comfort me. It was definitely a positive thing. I felt good about it. I don't know what else to say about it."

Back to your story...

"After about a year of him staying with us over the weekends, my boyfriend moved in with me."

Did he just decide to do so like your ex-husband? That's how it sounds. Explain how it came to this.

"I think it was quite different. First, this didn't happen in the first months of our relationship. It only happened after dating for more than a year. Second, it was a mutual desire and decision. We both wanted to move in together. So, no, he didn't just move in with me.

"Until that time, he had had his own business. Unfortunately, he didn't make any money and had built up a few debts. But he had found a regular job, which wasn't too far from where I lived. We were really happy together, and all seemed to be going well."

I don't hear you saying that you loved him being with you, just that it was convenient because he got a job close by.

"That's a strange thing to say. You're almost implying that I didn't love him, but let him move in because he managed to get a job close to where I lived. That doesn't make much sense. I did love him very much, and I loved being with him. That didn't have anything to do with him getting a job close by. We had a pretty good and happy life. Apart from my earliest childhood, that was the happiest time of my life up to then."

Well, I wanted you to share your thoughts with me. Not that I don't know them, but I wanted you to say it, because you need to be totally clear why you did certain things.

"A year later, we had the chance to buy a house together. The only obstacle was that he had a few debts from his studies, his car, and his business that needed to be paid off before we could get a mortgage. As I had a little bit of money, I decided to pay off his debts so we could go ahead with the purchase of the new house.

"My boyfriend insisted we see a solicitor to put it all into an agreement and make sure I'd get the money back if we'd ever split up."

So, did you go and get a contract?

"Yes, we did end up getting a contract that was mainly created to protect my finances. After that was signed, we could purchase our new home. We were very happy to move into our new home. Then, just a week after we moved in, I got sick. At first, I thought it had all been a bit much, the moving, working, the kids. I was very tired, was having migraines, and had to vomit four or five times a day. I thought it would go away with a bit of rest, but 2 weeks later, I still didn't feel any better at all."

Why are you suddenly sick? Did something happen out of the ordinary? Think about that.

"Apart from moving into a new house in another city, I was bitten by what I believe was a spider at the time of moving in. But even now, years later, I'm still not sure what caused me to be so sick.

"I went to see my new doctor, who couldn't find anything and suggested to stay at home for another week before returning to work. So I stayed home another week, but still nothing had changed. I felt really sick and wasn't able to do anything at all. Sometimes, I wasn't even able to make myself a cup of coffee. Other days, I felt reasonably well and could even manage to go to work for a few hours. This dragged on for a few weeks and months, but instead of getting better, I only felt sicker."

By then, your doctor should have developed some ideas what to do......

"Yeah, hahaha. Well, I'm laughing, but not really because after talking to my doctor, he suggested that I didn't want to work and pretended to be sick to get out of working. I was furious. I wasn't pretending anything; I really felt very sick.

"I tried to still do as much as I could, and some days, I was sick but felt all right to work for a few hours. Other times, I felt so sick that I couldn't even get up.

"On those days, my daughters, who were 10 and 8 years old at the time, had to make their own breakfast, their own lunch, and, sometimes, even their own dinner.

"Unfortunately, my boyfriend wasn't much around. He often had to travel for work and sometimes wasn't home for days. I felt guilty, because I wasn't there to take care of my girls and to be with them. Some days, I wasn't even able to go to the living room and lay on the sofa.

"My doctor, who still didn't believe anything was wrong, sent me to the hospital for some testing, which didn't turn up with anything at all. He also sent me to see a psychiatrist. My doctor thought it was all in my head and that, for some reason, I was making it up. The psychiatrist sent me home after three sessions. There wasn't anything wrong, at least not on a mental level, apart from being distressed about being sick and no one believing me."

I still don't understand the reason for this sudden change from running two shows at a time to not being able to cope with basic things. You need to think through this better.

"I don't understand why you're saying this. I still don't understand what was happening and why I was so sick. Am I missing something?"

You are missing something, and one day, you'll find out what it was. It wasn't just one single thing. I know you're already getting a better understanding, but you have some more digging to do.

"Why can't you just tell me what was going on? Don't you know?"

I sure do know, but it's important that you truly understand this, and you'll only be able to do that if you discover for yourself what has happened. Again, I'm not here to explain life or to give you all the answers you're seeking. I'm here to help you make sense of your past and to guide you in the right direction. What I'm simply saying here is that you're getting closer to answers. You only have to dig a little deeper. So don't give up.

"Well, that's not fair. Why can't I have answers right now?"

Oh, oh, are you being impatient yet again?

"Alright, I'll let it go…for now at least. Let me continue my story. A friend gave me the number of a private clinic in Amsterdam that specialized in food allergies and chronic fatigue. By that time, I'd been sick for over 1½ years and felt pretty desperate. It turned out that I was allergic to 149 of the 175 foods they tested, and I had to go on a very strict diet.

"I had to go to the clinic every week and usually had to catch public transport because I felt too sick to drive. It was a pain because I couldn't get there without having to vomit at least once. One day, my boyfriend took a few hours off work to drive me and we had to stop two times because I was throwing up. I think it was only then that he realized that I really wasn't well at all.

"My boyfriend's mother suggested that if no one could help, I still had the ability to heal myself. I was a bit puzzled when she suggested that I could heal myself. When I asked her how I could do that, she said that I would know myself how to do that. I thought about what she had said for a while but didn't really understand what to do. However, I did enroll in a meditation course, the Da Silva technique, which is a very deep form of meditation. I was hoping that that could help.

"For the next few months, I meditated three times a day and kept to a very strict diet. Slowly, very slowly I started to feel a bit better. It took a long time, and a strict diet and routine, but I did get a lot better. Not at once, but little by little. I'm not sure if it was the meditation or the diet, or both."

That's good news, I think. And now you're fine again? Are you?

"I know that I haven't recovered 100%; maybe 80% would be more accurate. There are times—thank God hardly ever—when I get that same feeling again with severe migraines, extreme fatigue, and vomiting. The fatigue has never really disappeared, but, at least, today, I can function at some level. When I get those severe headaches again and start vomiting, I know that I need to slow down and meditate more, watch what I'm eating, and take better care of myself."

You were pretty sick back then and yes, when you're too busy or under too much stress, when your immune system is down, you're likely to get it back.

But it's good that you now recognize the first signs and that you're able to take action before it becomes a real problem again.

You've learned to listen to your body a lot better, and you've learned that you can help heal your own body. The thing is that you should do that a lot more than you're doing right now. You're still tired, and still not totally healthy, but, often, you push it away and go on with your busy life.

"Yes, you're right, I try to go on with normal life as much as I can because if I didn't, I wouldn't have a life at all. I'm exhausted, but I can't let that stop me from living my life as best as I can. Anyway, I still don't know what was really wrong with me at the time."

Stop for a second before going on. Did you listen to what I was saying? I said that you've learned to listen to your body and you've learned that you can help heal your own body. The thing is that you should do that a lot more than you're doing right now.

"Yes, I know that. It just seems that there's never time for these things. Life goes so fast. I'm hardly keeping up. There's always so much to do. And, I still don't know what was really wrong with me."

Okay, I'll let you have it your way and give you some input that can help you to find the answers. I think at some level, you do know what happened, but, okay, I'll tell you. Yes, you had food allergies and chronic fatigue. This was triggered by a spider bite and a virus. You still carry this virus, which may seem dormant but isn't. You have it in an advanced stage. It was also caused by something else that triggered it. You haven't talked about it yet. I understand. Again, it's not something very common and it's weird, just to use your own words.

"You mean that what has to do with the circles that I saw on my window?"

Yes, exactly. On a completely other level, this has made an impact too. Tell me what happened.

"True, this is another "weird" thing that has happened. Do I really have to talk about that? I'm not very keen."

I understand. Look, I'm not here to tell you what to say or what not to say. I already know what you're going to say anyway. But, do you remember why we're having this conversation?

"Uh, yes. We're having this conversation so that I can get clear on my past, understand what has happened, and move on with more clarity, understanding, and focus.

"Okay then, here I go..."

Reflection:

- There's no such thing as coincidence.
- There's no shame in asking for help.
- You can't help everyone, but helping just one person does make a difference, if only for that one person.
- Meditation is a great stress reliever.

The Magic Of A Different Reality

***

"Remember how I told you about the seven circles I saw on my window?"

Yes...?

"Well, I did see them again, sort of. When I was so sick, the only thing I could cope with was watching a bit of TV now and then. One day, I was watching a program, and it was talking about a psychic boy, a teenager, who had seen UFOs and crop circles.

"Of course, I had to watch this, especially when they showed pictures of circles. They weren't crop circles, but some type of see-through circles that were dancing in the air. They looked exactly the same as the circles I had seen on my window!

"Yes, absolutely, I was intrigued. Maybe now I was going to get some answers. According to this boy, the circles were a type of energy being. Unfortunately, I only started watching at the end of the program, and, before much more was said, the program ended. I didn't know who this boy was; I didn't know anything more about these circles. The only thing I really found out was that I wasn't the only one seeing it.

"I wanted to get in contact with this boy and talk to him about his experience and tell him about mine. Maybe he was able to make more sense out of it. Maybe he knew what they were. I tried to find out more online, but the only thing I could find out was that the program was a repeat, and that it had been on the air before."

Why are you making such a fuss about something that probably doesn't mean anything at all? Probably, it's just another person seeing circles that were caused by light reflection.

"I understand why you're saying this because that's what I had thought at first. But if you're seeing it every morning for weeks and weeks, and if you can't wipe it away, then I believe it's a bit more than just an optical illusion.

"Anyway, I talked about it with my then boyfriend, and he said to me, 'this is really important to you, isn't it?' I couldn't deny it. Yes, it was very important to me. I told him that I had been trying to find out more, but that I had hit a dead end. He then said that if it were really important, something would happen.

"He was right! Something did happen! The next morning, I found the local newspaper on my doorstep, and it had a picture of this boy on the front page!"

Unbelievable.

"Are you sarcastic now?"

Hmmm. Just teasing you.

"Unbelievable, like you said, but true. There was a picture and a whole article about him and about his experiences. I felt that I needed to get in contact with him. I contacted the local paper, and found out his phone number via the editor. When I called the boy and explained why I wanted to meet him and talk to him, he agreed. We set a date and time, and a few days later, we met at his parents' house. I felt excited, but also very nervous."

Why? Why did you feel so nervous?

"Uhm. It still was strange for me to talk about these types of things. Yes, I've seen it, I've experienced it, but, at the same time, I also know that most people don't have such experiences. Or if they do and they're like me, they don't talk about them."

So you're still nervous and unsure, even though this boy has had a similar experience, been on TV and in the paper, and has publicly shown pictures of the circles you've seen as well?

"Yes, that's right. I still sometimes doubt myself. And I guess that I have trouble accepting these things. I always try to explain things from a logical and rational point of few, but in these cases, I can't. It sometimes makes me wonder if I'm actually seeing it, feeling it, knowing it."

Really, do you now really still doubt yourself?

"Yes, I do. From a pure rational point, I still doubt myself. And yet..."

And yet...?

"And yet, it's happening, I'm seeing, feeling, and knowing things. I'm not hallucinating or making things up. But, even though it's my reality and it's real to me, I wonder sometimes if it truly is reality, if it really happened."

Okay, I understand how you feel, but for the moment, let's move on. Tell me what happened next.

"I went to see him, and I told him my story about the circles I had seen on my window. He told me where he had seen these circles. It was out in an open field close to some trees, not far from where he lived. He showed me some pictures of it. I looked at them and recognized them. These circles he had photographed looked the same as the circles I had seen myself. I asked him if he thought it had any meaning, and his reply was that they were a different life form. They were kind and gentle energy beings. That made sense to me. That was what I had felt as well.

"He then asked if I had any other experiences that were "out of the ordinary." I told him about the vision I had had about the UFO and the aliens who told me I wasn't from here. He looked at me and, after some time, he said, 'I believe there's a connection between you and a different world. Let me show you some pictures I took. Maybe you recognize something.'

"Over the next half hour, he showed me pictures of crop circles that appeared on an agriculture field right behind his parent's house. He had so many pictures. But they didn't do too much for me. I looked at them, but they were just pictures. Until….

Until?

"Until he showed a new pile of pictures. One of them caused a huge reaction on my side. I don't know what happened, but my breathing became very fast and the hairs on my arms were standing up. I became really excited, almost upset after seeing this picture."

Why?

"I don't know why. I didn't get a reaction with any of the other pictures. I have no idea why I got such a reaction seeing this one.

The boy said that there obviously was a connection between me and that crop circle. He said that it confirmed his feeling that my vision of the UFO could be more than just a vision.

"This meeting confirmed to me that I wasn't seeing things. But, unfortunately, it still didn't explain anything. Still there was no reasoning, no logic behind it, just someone who had the same type of experience. I met with him one more time, but nothing else happened. And then I moved to Australia, and that was the end of it."

How do you normally feel about these experiences? I mean, I understand you think they're weird, but do you feel concerned, scared, or happy? How do you feel about them?

"In general, I feel good about them. They're mostly positive experiences. The only negative experience I had was the one I had as a child when I saw angry spirits coming through the wall of my bedroom."

That's good. I'm happy you have mainly good experiences.

Can you tell me about your most positive "weird" experience or vision?

"Yes, I'd love to tell you about it. It was absolutely wonderful. It still brings a broad smile to my face and it still warms my heart, in a way it has never been warmed before.

"I had a vision. Again, I know this was a vision because everything was crystal clear. There was nothing blurry about it and I still remember to this day although it must have been more than 20 years ago when I had this vision.

"I'm on another planet. It's a beautiful planet with blue-green, aqua colors. And it's full of love. I feel love inside of me and all around me. It's so warm, such a total Love that I feel. The planet is pure Love, the surroundings are pure Love, and the colors are pure Love... I look up and see another being standing opposite me on my left side. This being doesn't have clear features. I can make out the outlines of a head and body, but that's about it. The being is white, with golden yellow around the belly area. Then I realize that I also am a being of this kind. I look the same. I'm surprised; I'm not human. The feeling is incredible. I feel an overwhelming love for my companion, and I can feel "its" love for me. It's happy, beautiful, and intense. The feeling of Love is so intense that the yellow in the area of our bellies starts to bubble, like yellow golden bubbly champagne.

"Next, I see this yellow golden champagne forming a string coming out of our bellies and connecting in the middle. It's such a beautiful vision and such a beautiful feeling. It's pure Love. It connects in the middle and then it starts forming another loving being. I'm overwhelmed. It's so beautiful. There's so much Love. It's absolutely Divine. We've just created another soul.

"It isn't just this new being that's Divine, but all is Divine; all is Love, all is heavenly beauty: us, our surroundings, the new being we created, absolutely everything. I feel like I'm totally surrounded, submerged in Love. Love is both outside and inside of me. It's an experience more beautiful and touching than anything else I've ever experienced.

"I realize that our souls have connected to create. I look around me and the colors are so intense, as intense as the love I feel. This is what real Love feels like. No conditions, no fear, only strong golden yellow bubbly Love. I realize that Love isn't created because we exist, but instead that Love creates Existence (of new life).

It was the most wonderful, beautiful, intense experience ever. You cannot imagine how much Love there was. Nothing that we experience here on earth can compare to it."

I know that this is the most intensive experience you've ever had. This beats anything else. The Love your experienced in your vision is much more powerful and far more intense than what humans understand love to be. How did you feel after this vision?

"First, I felt really, really happy, then I felt truly sad, and then I felt happy again."

I understand the happiness, but I don't understand why you felt so sad. Can you explain that?

"Yes, I will. I felt sad because I had never experienced this type of intense overwhelming love here on earth. It was so beautiful that I felt like crying. I felt sad because we humans don't feel this love."

So you're saying we humans don't love the same way?

"Not sure if you can say that, but human love doesn't feel as intense as what I had experienced in that vision. And that makes me sad. I would like everyone to experience that. There would no longer be any need for hate, anger, fear, or war. That Love provided for everything these beings needed to live, unlike humans."

Almost sounds like paradise.

"Yes, you're right."

I can understand you felt sad that you don't feel that Love being a human being, so why were you happy again then?

"I realized something. I realized that the core of that Love, the source, is also in every human being. But often, if not always, we have trouble fully accessing it, or we totally forget about it. Let me try to explain what I mean by that.

"Loving fully, like those beings on that other planet do, requires letting go of fear, of anger, of hate and all these things. To me, it also looks like letting go of control. I think human beings want to have control, and that control blocks true Love. When we completely, unconditionally Love, then there's no need for control, fear, anger, and so on.

"So, for example, in our fear of getting hurt, we defend ourselves; we build a wall around our Love. And this wall prevents Love to show, to come out completely. It also prevents us from receiving love. I believe it's there; it's in all of us, but we just don't always access it."

That's interesting. What can we do to change that?

"I suppose the first step to change is to become aware. We can't change anything we're not aware of, at least not intentionally. I don't know though how we can all become aware. I can't make everyone have that same vision. More than that, even when we would be aware, that still doesn't necessarily change anything. Although I'm aware, I have not suddenly become a more loving person. Probably because I still have fears, I still get angry, and I most certainly don't like losing control (if there's truly such a thing as control).

"Feeling that type of Love may be a process, a change of attitude that may take up many years or many lifetimes. But we can all make an effort at making a move toward it, trying to be kinder, more loving, every day, trying to be a better person. I'm not saying that this will never happen. I'd like to believe that it will happen. I would love for every single person to experience that Love, if not our generation, then maybe future generations. If there's anything I want to pray for, then that is it!

"It has certainly made a change in my life in the sense that I try to be more loving, more understanding, and helpful."

I can see this has made a lasting impression on you. Thank you for sharing that.

Let's move on. You've had other visions that include aliens, and I would like you to talk about it.

"Yes, you're right. There were other visions with aliens. God knows why that's happening. Why can't I keep it simple and more realistic and just dream normal dreams about humans?

"But okay, here's the next vision… I'm in a flight control tower, and I can look around me and see planes landing and taking off. A door opens, and I see Almira entering. I'm pleasantly surprised. It's such a pleasure to meet her again. She was the woman who was with me when I saw the UFO when I was 5 years old. We hug, and then she explains what she wants from me. She tells me that a bit later, a spaceship with aliens will come to meet us. She is the negotiator on the alien side, I have been appointed to negotiate on behalf of the humans. We have been chosen because both the aliens and the humans trust that we will make the right decisions. I feel honored and humbled, but also the pressure and importance of doing a good job, a job that's for the benefit of all, a job of which I don't consciously have all the details. I don't even know what the negotiations are about.

"Then the sky opens up. So strange. The colors, the outlines of the clouds, the tower, and everything is so clear. There's a clear outline of where the sky opens up, and through this hole in the sky, a spaceship appears. The next moment, several aliens appear in the tower, and we all sit down at a long oval boardroom table. We talk without words. We can all read each other's minds. I'm aware that a decision is being made and that all parties are happy. However, I'm not consciously aware of the actual decision. The decision was made on a subconscious level. I don't know what the decision was, it could have been anything. I do have a good feeling though, and I'm happy with the result even though I don't remember what the result of the meeting was.

"We say our goodbyes, and then the aliens and UFO disappear as quickly as they appeared. It felt like the whole thing didn't even last five minutes."

Do you know what it means, if it means anything at all?

"No, I truly have no idea. I can speculate, but that doesn't necessarily make it true. I can only say it left me with a good feeling. I felt like I had accomplished something very important, and seeing Almira again made me very happy."

Okay, I believe you when you say that you have no idea what it means. Although we would all like to have all our questions answered, sometimes, we're not ready to receive the answer.

"Uh? Are you saying I'm not ready to understand the meaning of this vision?"

Yes, that's what I'm saying. Don't worry, there's nothing wrong with it. Everything has its own time. Events, answers to questions, they all find a place when the time is right.

"Hmm. I can't say I really like that. I would like to have answers now."

Hahaha. Here you go again. You can be very patient with other people, but you're most certainly not too patient with yourself.

"I don't need to be patient with myself. It doesn't have anything to do with this. I just want answers to my questions. I want to know why I have these visions and what they mean. Is that too much to ask for?"

No, the question is fair and relevant. The answer, however isn't something that you would be able to handle or comprehend at this moment.

So, before we get into an argument…let's talk about another vision you had. Yes, again, one with aliens.

"I don't understand why I have these visions about aliens. It's so strange, yet, at the same time, so normal. I never seem to be feeling scared or even uncomfortable engaging with aliens in my visions. It's all so natural.

"In another vision, a very short one, I'm in an abandoned building, garage, or bunker. It's old and broken down, and it's dark inside and outdoors.

Actually, this is the first vision with aliens, where I don't feel completely comfortable and safe.

"There are many different alien species with me. There are the Greys and the Greens as we know, and another species that look very much like them but are a bit rounder and fatter. Their color is beige and dark brownish red. I call them the Mêlées. I'm not so familiar with them, but we seem to have established some kind of mutual respect and acceptance. One of them comes up to me and shakes my hand. I'm happy that we've been able to put our mistrust aside and are able to build toward a future relationship.

"While we are exchanging some words—well not really words, but merely conversation through telepathy—there suddenly is some turmoil. When I look up, my eye catches some movement outside of the building. I see yet another alien species, and I instantly understand that I have to be very careful. This species cannot be trusted. They're dangerous. This one looks like an oversized insect, like a gigantic cockroach, about twice my size. From the reaction of the other aliens in the building, I understand that they too are afraid of this being. And, I understand that, although I may have been able to build positive relationships with some of the alien species, this large cockroach-like being will not be one of them, or, at least, not for now.

"It was a short vision many years ago, but I still remember it very clearly. It left me with mixed feelings. I felt like I had only partly succeeded. That doesn't make too much sense, as I don't even know what I had to accomplish in the first place. But anyway, yes, I had yet another vision, another encounter with aliens."

I understand you've several visions or experiences with beings from other worlds. Thank you for having the guts to share that. I understand that you normally never talk about these things, not even with the people in your life whom you trust. I understand that you don't talk about it because a part of you still doesn't understand…But, one day, you will. Let's leave it at that.

"How do you know that I'll understand one day? You're me and I'm you. If you know this today, then I should also know it today. Why do we share the same knowledge, but then don't know the same. You need to explain this to me."

It's very simple. Actually, the human body is very complicated, but the answer to your question is simple. It's simple when you understand that you're here to learn and to evolve. You can access the answer by going to the "library" and read the appropriate "books." You're very intuitive, so you'll find the answer to your question.

As I've said here before, I'm here to guide you and to make sense of your past; I'm not here to provide you with all the answers that you can look up in the "library." Question for you: are you accessing the information in the library often enough? The answer is "No." So, there you go. I've now given you the next steps to find the answer yourself. As any good teacher, I'm teaching you to look for answers yourself instead of spelling it all out.

Getting back to your visions, I'd also like you to share another vision that you had, where you were called the Messenger.

"Hmmm, yes, okay, I will. I love this vision.

"I'm sitting on a chair, and all of the sudden, I feel a bit sleepy and slightly dizzy. It's as if I'm zooming out and, for a very short moment, all is black. Then I find myself sitting in another chair, in another room, in a different time. I talk with the people in the room, just a bit of chitchat. What we talk about is just some polite talking, like talking about the weather. But my reason for being there, as I understand it, is to deliver a message. I don't know what the message is, I'm only the messenger. I don't know if the message came written in an envelope or through some other means. It isn't important. What's important is that I did deliver the message, which is of great interest and importance.

"Then I get sleepy and dizzy again and before I know it I'm sitting in another chair, in a different room. The same things happen; I know I have delivered an important message of which I don't know the contents. I realize that this is yet another here and now.

"The same thing happens about seven times. Every time I'm in a different place in a different time. I go to the middle ages as well as to the industrial era and to the future, and other times and places."

That's the very first time you mention going to the future. It was always going to the past up to now. Is it different to go to the future?

"No, it doesn't make a difference. In my visions, it just happens, and it's totally normal. In the vision I don't understand why, or how I am going to other times and places, or what is going on. It just happens; I don't control it.

"But then I sit down again, and focus on making it happen myself. Guess what? It works. I can create that same feeling again, black out for a split second, and find myself in another place and time. And then I start doing this repeatedly. I may not know the message, but it's important that the same message gets out to as many places as possible. I am the Messenger dedicated to delivering the message."

That was a very important vision. You'll have to discover for yourself what it really means. You'll understand when the time is right.

"Yes, you have said that a few times now. I find your comments very frustrating. Why can't you just explain to me why I'm having these visions with aliens? Are you not explaining them because you believe I'm making them up?"

No, you're not making them up. You're just not ready to hear the answer. However, you'll understand more and more in the coming time. You'll write about it in your next book.

"What? I have no intention to write another book, let alone explaining why I have those visions."

Believe me, you'll start to understand, and you'll write again. You're even going to mention this further on in this book.

Now, let's talk about something different. Let's get back to earth in the here and now as we know it.

Reflection:

- There are many things we cannot explain (yet), but that doesn't make it any less of a reality. Is the wind an illusion?
- Love is The Creative Force, The Source or God.
- Real Love doesn't know fear, anger, or control, and is unconditional.
- We can only change that of which we're aware.

Australia, Here I Come

***

Let me give you a break. Let's leave the "weird and alien" stuff behind. Let's talk about Australia and what happened in those first two years. That, at least, wasn't "weird," using your own words. You moved from the Netherlands to Australia. Tell me about it...

"At the time my boyfriend got a job offer from a company in Australia. He had done some work for a Dutch company, and this Australian company was a client of that Dutch company. The first time he went over to Australia in 1997, he came back home really enthusiastic. He told me that he wanted to go and live in Australia.

"I wasn't against or for it. I just hadn't been there and wanted to get a feel about Australia before making the decision to move."

What are you saying? You didn't jump on it? You got the chance to discover another country and you were careful?

"Yes."

What had changed? Earlier you would have said yes without even thinking twice about it.

"I guess my situation had changed. I was no longer just by myself. I now had a family I needed to take care of. I may want whatever I want, but, in the end, it was no longer just about me. I suppose you can say that I wanted to make sure we could make it work."

There's another reason why I'm surprised you didn't jump on it. It has to do with something that happened when you were about 17 years old.

"Oh yes, I forgot about that....My parents received a postcard from one of their friends who went on a holiday to Australia. It had a picture of the Opera House on it. I remember looking at the postcard and telling my parents that, one day, I'd live there in Australia. It took another 20 years, but yes, I did end up living in Australia.

"A few weeks after my boyfriend told me he wanted to move to Australia, I got the opportunity to get an idea of what living in Australia could be like. My boyfriend had to go back. As he felt so strongly about wanting to live there, I took two weeks off work to be able to go with him, and experience Australia myself. Not that you can truly experience any other country in two weeks, but at least I could get a feel for it and get a first impression.

"I loved it! I totally understood why he wanted to move. And we soon decided to see if we could make that idea a reality. In the next year, while he was travelling to Australia several more times, I started the migration process. We were in no rush, but were going to slowly get our paperwork in order, so that we could move as soon as we felt we were ready.

"That moment came when he got a job offer from that Australian company. As our migration process wasn't finalized yet, this company arranged for a business visa that would allow him to work. That, of course all didn't happen overnight. We had to be patient. Finally we stepped on a plane starting our big adventure.

"My daughters had mixed feelings. My older one was excited, my younger one wasn't so happy. She didn't like leaving her friends behind. Although we had tried to build a positive picture and presented it as an adventure and something new, some family members and friends weren't all that positive, and they left a few not so realistic ideas in the girls' heads.

"Some of them said, 'Australia? Why would you want to live there? It's a hot desert.' Others said, 'You wouldn't like it. You're country girls, not city girls.' A lot of people had opinions, although none of them had ever been there."

How did that make you feel?

"Well, it's not nice of people trying to influence kids in a negative way. I believe some people were jealous of us, and others were just not as adventurous and simply couldn't imagine someone taking as big a step as we took.

"I get that. Not everyone is the same and some people may really not understand why someone else leaves to live in another country. I get that everyone is different and that some people live in the same place and work for the same company all of their lives. Other people move around and live in different countries. That's fine. What isn't fine is to scare children."

Hmm. Didn't you do the same? Didn't you scare your daughters by moving to the other side of the world?

"No, I don't think I did. I tried to explain it very well. I tried to explain what they could expect, and they knew they always would have me with them. It's one thing to present it as an adventure. It's another thing to make it a big scary thing."

I know you don't always like me to ask this, but what did your mother say?

"My mother wasn't happy, and she tried to talk me out of it, but we had made up our minds, and there was no stopping us. Someone had told my mother that I wouldn't stay in Australia and that I'd be back in the Netherlands in 2 years. Maybe that comforted her in some way. I don't know."

And your sister?

"My sister didn't try to talk me out of it, but I know that she found it hard. We're very close, and maybe she thought that we would never see each other again. I believe by now she has accepted the fact that I'll stay here in Australia, and I think she understands why. I know that if she could, she'd love to come over and live here as well. She's been over to visit us many times, and she loves it here."

But it didn't all turn out the way you had planned it, did it?

"No, not exactly. Although my boyfriend had a reasonably good income, we didn't count on living in Australia being so expensive. The normal cost of living is much higher than in the Netherlands. That was a bit of a shock.

"On top of that, it took a while before we could sell our house in the Netherlands. And, because people knew we wanted to sell quickly, as we had moved overseas, we didn't get as much for it as we had hoped."

"And then, of course, I didn't work. So we lost our second income. It wasn't that I didn't want to work. It was a conscious decision to stay at home for the first year and help my daughters with school. As they didn't speak any English when we arrived, they needed a bit more help during that first year. That was fine. It was a decision that was made upfront, and I still believe it was the right decision.

"However, we had a lot less income than we were used to. And, all together, money was pretty tight."

And getting back to work also wasn't so easy, was it? You thought you would be able to easily get a good job back in IT, but the reality of it turned out to be a big struggle.

"After the first year in Australia, I was ready to go back to work. The kids were doing fine and were even starting to correct my English. They had made new friends, and were really doing very well. I think I can say that they both had adapted well and were enjoying living in Australia.

"Unfortunately, getting work wasn't as easy as I had expected. There were several factors that played a role."

Explain to me.

"It was just after the terrorist attacks of September 11, 2001, the IT industry went down and jobs were harder to get. I also was a migrant with no working experience in Australia, and I had been at home without working for over a year. These weren't very good conditions to get back into the workforce.

"After many unsuccessful attempts to get work, I decided to do a coaching training course. I thought that this was something I could do really well, given my background in facilitating training and my logical, rational mind, and love for working with people. That was a good decision. It gave me something to focus on and I didn't feel so useless. I loved the training course as well, and met some nice people.

"Around that time, the relationship with my boyfriend had hit rock bottom. I had more and more reason to believe that he could be homosexual or bi-sexual. Things weren't good."

Whoa! Stop right there. Are you saying you separated because you thought he was gay?

"No, not at all. That wasn't the main reason, but yes, it did play a roll. "His mother came over to visit us, and, instead of holding my hand and walking next to me, he was holding his mother's hand, and I had to walk behind them. Then I saw them kissing each other full on the mouth. I was grossed out. I didn't think that was normal. One of my girls saw it too and she too didn't think it was appropriate."

Well, sorry to say, but, to me, that doesn't make him gay or bi-sexual.

"No it doesn't. You're right. But it was just another contributing factor."

Contributing to what?

"It contributed to my feeling that something was going on, or not quite right. Then he had some issues at work. The company didn't do so well and he lost his job. Fortunately, he got a new job pretty soon afterwards and left for a few months to work overseas. When he came back, he told me that one of his male colleagues ended up in bed with another male colleague. He was so full of it and was telling me the story repeatedly, that I was starting to wonder if it had been him, instead of someone else.

"At the same time, he also started to act very strange. I found out that he had opened another bank account just for himself. He had taken money out of our joint accounts and transferred it to his new account. When I talked to him about it, his answer was that I had been acting very strange and that he thought I would walk away with all the money.

"Then a few days later, I wanted to make some online payments, and I could no longer get access to our joint accounts. The password had changed. When he came home, I confronted him. He didn't deny anything and asked me if I wanted him to leave. I answered yes, I had had enough of it, and it looked like he wanted out as well. So, he packed his things, walked out of the door, and was gone.

"Going to the bank to get access to the bank accounts, I discovered that there was only $750 left. All the rest had been transferred out of our joint accounts to the new account that he had opened.

"I was also not able to contact him. I tried and tried to find him, but without any results. He had disappeared, leaving me with not only very little money, no job, and two teenagers to take care off but also a credit card debt.

"After a month, I still hadn't been able to contact him. I realized that he didn't want to be found. Having no job, the little money left was gone in no time. But I wasn't too worried just yet. When we bought a house together in the Netherlands, we had made up a contract by a solicitor. Back then, I had paid off all my boyfriend's debts, and paid the deposit for the house. The contract stated that he would have to pay that amount back to me if we were ever to end our relationship. All together that amount was over AUD $80,000, a lot of money, especially when you don't have any.

"When following that up, I found out that in Australia, this contract wasn't valid because it was made up by one solicitor and not confirmed by another solicitor; both my boyfriend and I should have had our own solicitors. In other words, I never saw one single cent of that money!"

How did you feel about that? It doesn't seem fair.

"I felt relieved and betrayed at the same time. I felt relieved because I no longer had to live with someone who obviously didn't love me and didn't want to be with me. I felt betrayed because he left me without any financial means, and he didn't have to pay me back the money that was defined in the contract that we signed back in The Netherlands. That was money that I had worked for so hard after my divorce."

But that wasn't the only thing that hurt you. When he left, he did something else, didn't he?

"Yes, he had been spreading lies. When I called my best friend to tell her that he had left, she told me she already knew. She said to me that she no longer wanted to have any contact with me. When I asked why, she answered that he had told her that I had taken all money out of our bank account and had put it onto a new account that I had opened. She didn't want to be friends with anyone who would do something like that.

"I tried to explain to her that that wasn't true, and that it was just the other way around, but she didn't want to listen and hung up the phone."

Again, your friends betrayed you after a break up. I know that that has been very painful. It has been another contributing factor for you having issues trusting other people. Can you tell me about the first time that your friends let you down?

"The first time was after I divorced my husband and when I got to know my boyfriend. The contact with my friends was getting less and less, and although I made an effort to keep in contact, it was hard because that was around the time that I got sick, and we lived on the other side of the country.

"When one of our friends died in a car accident, I realized that they were no longer my friends. At the funeral, I was totally ignored. When I tried to start a conversation with my friends, they just walked away. It was really hurtful and strange.

"Weeks later, I had the chance to talk to two of my oldest friends, and they told me that now that I was divorced and had a new boyfriend, they no longer wanted to be friends. I was living too far away and as the majority of the group of friends were old friends of my ex-husband, they decided to no longer have contact with me. That hurt, especially I felt like my best friend had let me down. She married my ex-husband's best friend, and I think it now became clear where her alliance was."

How has this affected you?

"What do you mean?"

Tell me about the friends you have right now.

"Well, uh… To be honest, I don't really have any friends at all. There are people I know and like, but it's not that I have friends I hang out with. I don't have a girlfriend I have coffees with or go to the movies with. The friends I have are mutual friends I have with my now husband. They're all people I've met at church, colleagues of my husband, or family of my sons-in-law. Like I said, they're lovely people, but they're not friends in the sense that we would hang out with them on a regular basis. We do invite them over now and then, but it's not like we would see each other often outside of main events.

"There's a couple who live about 500km south of us, and we visit them maybe once or twice a year. I love them dearly, but they're too far away to have regular contact."

So what are you going to do about that? Not having friends isn't good.

"I guess I have to join a club or something to meet new people, and I have to learn how to trust again. All I can say at this moment is that that's going to take some time."

It's fine if that takes some time, but you need to make more of an effort. Can you promise me to do that?

"Okay, yes, although that won't be easy, I'll make more of an effort to make new friends and start trusting again."

Great. That's a promise.

Now, let's go back to the time that your boyfriend left you. What happened next?

"Fortunately, at that time, I was volunteering at a retirement village, and they offered me a full-time job as a caregiver. This didn't cover my expenses though. Pay was so bad that I wasn't even able to pay the rent with it. Centrelink (an Australian Government Department that provides social security payments and services) provided the rest of the money that I needed for the rent, food, and other costs. Altogether, it was only very little money, and I could hardly make ends meet. With two growing teenagers at home, it was a hard thing to do."

Did you ever succeed finding him again?

"Yes, I actually did find him after about 10 years, somewhere online.

By that time, I had moved on, and didn't really want to go after him. Life was still really stressful and I didn't want to put even more pressure and stress on myself by contacting him and a lawyer to try to get any money out of him.

"I had dealt with that period of my life; I was doing financially okay. But the biggest reason why I didn't take any action was that I knew it would cause me a lot additional stress in an already very stressful life."

Reflection

- **Trust your instincts.**
- **We all need friends.**
- **Without trust, there cannot be a real connection.**

The Working Struggle

***

I assume your situation changed at some stage, and I assume it had to do with you getting a better job. Would you like to share that with me?

"Yes, of course I will. I've shared so many things with you already. This subject is probably one of the easiest or least painful things to talk about. I'm curious, though; you ask me if I would like to share that with you. I thought you already know everything about me, as you know everything there is to know."

Yes, I do. Don't question that again now. I thought we were getting somewhere. I mainly asked you to tell your story to share it with your family and others that are interested in your life.

"Just checking…"

How did you feel about your work in the retirement village?

"I didn't really like the physical work. Not that I don't want to do it, but I'm simply not that strong. I always felt exhausted and the work was very tiring.

"However, I loved the contact with the people. They all became family. I listened to their stories and was amazed at what some of them went through or what they were facing there in the retirement village, because of their age and of declining health.

"I remember George, who was always very funny and clumsy as well. I used to say to him, 'Careful, George.' His standard answer would then be, 'And if you can't be careful, you'll need to push a baby carriage.' So funny. We

---

got along really well and we had great conversations. He was really sweet and certainly one of my favorites.

"And then there was this man who had been a doctor. He had dementia and Parkinson and needed quite a bit of care. One day, I was entering his room and found him in the shower for the third time that day. He didn't remember. While I was drying him off, I was suddenly touched by emotion. I felt so much love, so much respect, not necessarily for him personally, but for life itself. At that very moment this life of this resident so imperfect, created a perfect moment of harmony, appreciation, love, and respect in my heart.

"Another day, when I was putting on his shoes, he, all of the sudden, seemed to have a clear moment, and he said to me, 'Thank you for your loving nature.' In another moment, he told me that I should go and study medicine. He thought I would make a great doctor.

That's kind of funny, as I always said that if I could start all over, I would study medicine and become a doctor, or study some type of alternative medicine. He made me realize that life doesn't need to be perfect to still be valuable. At that time, I respected and valued life as it was.

"I also took care of a woman I really liked. We used to have long conversations, and she told me that in a next life, she would like to be my mother. Strangely enough, I agreed with her. It felt right.

I also admired her. She was always so positive. She was a real example of strength and positivity.

"One of the stories she told me was about when she was a spy in the Second World War. She and her brother were captured in Japan and transported to one of the war camps. One day, they were forced to stand on the same spot for a whole day. Her brother needed to go to the bathroom, but wasn't allowed. After hours and hours having to stand there at the same spot and not being allowed to go to the bathroom, his bladder burst and, sadly, he died. That must have been so hard on her. Seeing your sibling die in front of your eyes must be incredibly hard.

"At old age, she had severe arthritis and I knew she always was in a lot of pain, but she never complained. She was probably the most positive person I've ever met. It was always a beautiful day, the food was always so nice, and she always smiled. With her positive attitude, she made life better for a lot of people. Yes, she certainly made my life better as well. Up to today, thinking of her makes me smile. I admired her.

"One day, the daughter of one of the other residents said to me, 'I don't know how you do this work. I don't understand how you can be okay showering these old people with their ugly old bodies.' The resident answered: 'She doesn't mind, because she loves us all.' And she was right. I really felt so much love for them. I loved them all. I didn't mind their old bodies, scars, or wrinkles. I thought they were beautiful because to me they were all telling a story, the story of life.

"These memories still stand out, and now and then, I think of them.

What also really stood out was how lonely many of these residents were. At Christmas, the kitchen in the retirement village was closed, and a frozen meal was provided for those who didn't spend Christmas with family or friends.

"Thankfully, most of the residents didn't spend Christmas alone, but my heart broke for those who were left to sit alone. I remember one man in particular who was sitting alone in his room, just staring out of the window…"

Yes, I know that you really loved the residents of the retirement village and that you loved to interact with them. It seems to me as well that they contributed a lot to your well-being at the same time as you taking care of them.

"That's true. I felt loved and respected. As I said before, if it weren't for the physical hard work, then this would be the type of work—working with people—that I love to do. It's never a one-way street. I give and get back the same if not more. They were my family.

"Personal experiences as the above combined with the fact that the population is ageing and many elderly don't have a sufficient pension or retirement fund or life insurance to live a happy life, formed the idea of creating a website for pensioners. The idea is that people help people to become more self-sufficient and less reliant on government help. I believe that every single person, no matter their age, color, religion, or social status, deserves the right to a dignifying old age. The seniors of today were the ones who gave birth to us, raised us, made sacrifices for us, and worked to provide us with food and a roof over our heads. Now it's our turn to take care of them!"

I know that you worked very hard on that website, and it has come a long way. What's stopping you from finishing it and getting it out there?

"There are a lot of factors playing a role. First, I paid for the development of this website out of my own pocket, and, as I don't work at the moment, I don't know how to find the funding to market it. I also still have to do more testing, but I don't know where to find the time. There are so many other things I need to do. I know I should have plenty of time, but there's so much to do that I don't even know where to start at this moment. I have more or less decided to concentrate on this book first, and then tackle the next project, which may or may not be the website. And there's another reason why the development of this website has slowed down; I don't know how to market it. There are several ideas, but, again, it will take a lot of time and money, both of which I don't have too much at the moment."

So, are you going to let it go?

"No, the website will be completed and brought to market. I just don't know how and when just yet. It may take some time for me to pick that up again."

At that time, when working in a retirement village, this wasn't the only thing you were doing, was it?

"No, at the same time, I was working on setting up my own business and doing a course. I reckoned that with my experience, I could actually coach other people, so I did a personal and business coaching training course.

"I loved it. Helping other people to improve their lives is a great thing. And, honestly, every time, I learned something new myself as well from coaching other people and hearing about their dreams and struggles.

"I believe every person has something to say. They all have a story to tell. Some of these stories are absolutely amazing and inspiring.

"After the training course, I did some presentations in gyms and got a handful of clients from that. The start was slow, and I wasn't really making too much money. However, it was a great addition to my work in the retirement village, which paid a very low rate.

"I also organized a coaching booth at an event and invited other coaches I knew to co-share the booth to minimize the costs. The first year I did this there were only three coaches including me. The next year I had organized a group of 16 coaches. I organized the booth and put a roster together, I sorted out all the payments and did all the administration regarding this event.

"Apart from getting a few more clients, I also met many fellow coaches. One of the coaches wanted to work together with me. And, as he was more focused on business coaching and I more on personal coaching, we did decide to explore the idea a bit further."

You did end up working together, didn't you? But, in the end, it threatened your life and that of your daughters. To be honest, I don't understand why you actually decided to work with him, especially as I remember that you had an inkling that something wasn't right.

"Yes, that's right. I did have this feeling that something wasn't right, but I doubted my own intuition.

"The result was that I lost my business and everything I had worked so hard for. I trusted the wrong person....again. It was very frustrating. Again, I had trusted someone who had let me down in the end.

"After the debacle with my coaching friend, I got lucky and got a small IT contracting job for 6 weeks. I worked for two major banks in several

Australian cities as a contractor. Unfortunately, in the last week, I was fired. One of the tellers at the bank asked me if I could help with an elderly woman. She was Dutch and hardly spoke any English. The bank teller asked if I was willing to translate, so that she could understand what the woman was after.

"Of course, I translated, but when the bank manager found out, I was fired on the spot. Apparently, I wasn't allowed to translate.

I am not saying that this doesn't make sense. It just didn't seem really fair considering that I was asked to translate by an employee of the bank. Anyway, I was fired and without income…again.

"After this job, I got my taxi drivers license and drove a taxi. This certainly wasn't the greatest job, and I had to put in many hours to make a living out of it, but that's exactly what it did. I made a living, and it was enough to keep us going. I was very grateful for that."

I guess you met some very interesting people in this job.

"Yes, I met some wonderful people while I was driving a taxi. One moment really stands out to me. I started more and more to drive clients with a mental or physical problem as well as elderly people.

One young man whom I had to drive twice a week had both a mental and physical disorder. He also couldn't talk! What I did notice, though, was that as soon as he got in the car, he'd turn on the radio and sing. So, one day, I thought that if he couldn't talk but could sing, maybe we could have a conversation while singing. So I asked him in a singsong voice if he liked the music. He looked surprised, but then he smiled and sang back that yes, he really likes music.

"From that moment on, we had beautiful conversations together. He was perfectly able to have a meaningful conversation, just not by talking. I mentioned it to his caregivers, who were surprised, but promised to try singing to him too. That was a wonderful experience, which still deeply touches my heart.

"Another time, I was waiting in my taxi at a taxi stand close to a pub.

It was just after 3am in the morning. Not a great time, as that's when you normally get all the drunks who want to get home. From a distance, I saw a man approaching. His whole body was full of tattoos and piercings. I wasn't too happy and thought about driving away, but something stopped me from doing that.

"And then this man knocked on the window of the car. He said, 'Can you please take me home? Look I have plenty of money.' He showed two hundred dollars in his hand. I decided to give him a break and drive him. As soon as he got into the car, he thanked me. He said that not many taxi drivers would take him, and that he was very grateful that I did.

"He turned out to be an absolutely lovely guy. He was very polite and we had a nice chat. He told me how his mother raised him and his six siblings all by herself and that he finally had been able to save up enough money to buy his now elderly and sick mother a little house. He even showed me pictures. When I dropped him off at this place, he paid me double the fare. I refused, but he insisted I take it and buy a nice meal out for my daughters and myself."

That really touched your heart as well, didn't it?

"Yes, it did. I also felt guilty about judging him before knowing him. It was a good example of how you should never judge a book by its cover.

"I also drove a few famous people, film stars and other celebrities, but what I liked most was working for a council and driving the elderly and disabled to appointments. I actually became taxi driver of the month for the great service I delivered to the people I drove within that council.

"I not only got them to appointments or picked them up from shopping but I also made it a point to make sure that they got back into their house safely, and I often would carry their groceries inside. That wasn't a big thing to do, but I suppose when you get older or have a disability it isn't always an easy thing to do yourself.

"But working 7 days a week 12 hours a day took its toll, and one day, I crashed. I didn't crash the car as such, but I just couldn't get out of bed at 2:30am any longer. I was exhausted and totally overworked.

"Luckily after 3 months of not working and resting at home, I was then able to get a job managing an office of a small IT company. It didn't pay very well, but I was very happy with the job. Back in the Netherlands, I had studied Business Information Systems, and had worked in IT for over 10 years. So finally, I got back having a permanent job in IT. From then on, I was working in IT in different roles, for different companies.

"I was doing a lot better, and was even able to buy a small car. I had not had a car for the last 2½ years, and that hadn't been too easy, having kids who needed to go places. I remember driving in my car to work and feeling so grateful for both. I felt very rich and so incredibly happy that I was able to afford a car again and now had a steady job that earned enough to provide us with a roof over our head and enough food on our table.

"Then I lost my job. The company I worked for wasn't doing too well, and, as I was the last one joining the company, I was one of the first people to go. That wasn't good, as I was just starting to get back on my feet. I did, however, gain a lot of knowledge and experience. I then decided to start my own IT training and consulting company."

So, again you dived in, and started something completely different. Why are you doing that? It's almost when one thing doesn't work out, you start some kind of new adventure.

"Well, you're right to some extent. I like a lot of variety in my life, and it always excites me to do something different. But, in this case, it was also driven by the fact that I lost my job and needed to do something to earn money. I saw a gap in what other companies offered, and I filled it.

"I remember I made the decision around the end of June. By the end of August, I had developed several training programs in my company's business area. The next month, I started a marketing campaign, and in October, I facilitated the first training. This was only for two people from the same company and I didn't make a lot of money, but it was a good start.

"Then, a month later, I got a call that they wanted me to facilitate that same training course for a group of 24 people. Wow! Yes! That was great! I facilitated the training for that group of people and then once again to another group at the same company. They also engaged me on a 6-month consultancy contract, writing policies.

"From then on, I was presenting this training course about once or twice a month and had clients from different government departments, all the big banks, universities, building companies, and more."

You made good money and you traveled a lot from one city to another and all around Australia, and you also went to the USA. That's really you. You love to travel.

"Yes, I was on a roll for about four years traveling around, and then it kind of stopped. I didn't get any new work coming in. I hadn't changed my tactics, I didn't do anything different, but work slowed down so much that I needed to consider alternatives. With the IT world changing, the need for an expert in my area had decreased. At the same time, I was also getting a bit bored with what I was doing. Time after time, I would present the same content. That was getting boring for me. I felt that I wasn't learning anything new. I did form an alliance with another organization in the USA and for a long while, I thought about presenting their workshops. However, there wasn't enough money to be made. On top of that, I was working from home, and for days and days, I wouldn't really see any other living soul except for my husband and daughters. I was getting pretty lonely.

"Then, with the never ceasing support of my now husband, I got a contracting job as an IT Business Analyst at a large government project. Since then, I've had regular work, working on projects for several government departments and earning good money as a contractor..."

You got really stressed when you decided to wind down your company. Why was that?

"The only reason I was so stressed was because I didn't know when I'd be able to get a new job and make a living. That thought really scared me. I certainly didn't want to end up in poverty as I'd done before."

And how do you feel, now that you've had a constant flow of work and money coming in for several years? I'm asking because there's more to it. There's more to working. I understand that you don't really want to bring this up.

"Yes, you're right. How can I explain? I don't really want to bring it up because I feel ashamed for feeling so. It feels like I'm ungrateful.

"But, I hate it… I don't hate working as such, and I don't hate the work as a business analyst, but I hate trying to maneuver within all the politics and personal gain games that often go on at the cost of other people as well as business cost and, often, at a cost to the taxpayer.

"So, although I'm very grateful for the interesting and well-paying work, I find it harder and harder to deal with the politics."

What do you mean by "politics"?

"I mean, that a lot of people have their own agendas that aren't necessarily good for the company. Here in Australia, it doesn't seem that business is based on facts, logic, and honesty. Here, it's based, as I said, on politics, kingdoms, and queendoms, and little games people play. I absolutely hate that, and I have increasing issues dealing with that. In fact, it's causing a hell of a lot of stress.

"I'm a very straightforward person, and I've been told that I'm pretty direct. At a business meeting, I won't tell people what they want to hear; I refuse to play games. I'll contribute to serve the business in a rational way. I just cannot play these political games. This means that I'm often the one speaking up or speaking out even if that's against the general opinion of the people in the room. Or maybe many are of the same opinion, but are just too scared to speak up."

Maybe your approach is too rational. People like to hear what they like to hear, not what they need to hear.

"That's true. I'm learning to keep my big mouth shut, but that's hard to do, and even if I don't say anything, I still think it. It's stressful. It was so different in the Netherlands where it was important to speak up because coming up with other ideas and questioning things that didn't make sense contributed in better decision making and therefore a better business outcome. In the Netherlands, it's expected of you that you voice your opinion. Even if that opinion doesn't make sense, at the very least, it will start a healthy conversation to come to the best possible conclusion or outcome.

"Here in Australia, I know that, at least three times, my contract was cut short or not renewed because I was being too honest and open instead of being political. I just can't. I can't play games and manipulate. It goes against what I believe in."

But you decided to live in Australia. There's good and bad in every society. Maybe you can find a way to use your skills in a way that the people will appreciate. What do you think?

"Yes, you're right. I'm still learning to be diplomatic instead of blunt. It's not easy though. It's just very hard to have to work in an environment where I have a totally different mindset. It's very, very stressful every single day because I know I have to watch out for what I'm saying while at the same time I still want to contribute the best I can for the business and the clients of that business. Working for government departments also means that I'm working for the taxpayer. In the end, the taxpayers are paying for my salary, and I owe it to them to contribute the best way I possibly can. That makes me extra conscientious. It makes me feel that I have to do what's best for the business instead of playing political games.

"I find it very hard, and, to be honest, I don't know for how much longer I can do that. Having to deal in organizations with many people who have a total different work attitude is hard. I also always have to watch my back and I have to watch what I say. It's no fun at all."

Do you think this would be different in today's Netherlands?

"The Dutch society has changed a lot since I last lived there, so I don't know if the working environment and attitude has changed as well. It could well be, but I'm not sure.

"I just wish I could quit and do something different where my honest contribution is appreciated. That doesn't mean people always have to agree. It does mean that all ideas and opinions are taken into consideration for the best possible business outcome."

I know you've been struggling with this for a long time. And you now have decided to find a part-time job as business analyst, while at the same time working on something else. If you were to quit your full-time job, what would you like to do? Have you thought about that?

"Yes, I've thought about that many, many times. And I know that there are a few things I would love to do. However, I'm reluctant, because I know I probably wouldn't be earning as much, or maybe not at all. That's a problem for two reasons: I believe that in our marriage, I also need to contribute by earning money, and second, it will make me feel more dependent on my husband, and, with that, I would feel less in control. Also, I don't want to put extra pressure on him and making him the sole provider. I know how that feels. I just don't think that's fair.

"But okay, I'll share with you what I have been thinking about. My longtime view and wish is that I become a motivational speaker and entertainer. Wow, okay, now I've said it. I've never told anyone before. I would love to motivate and encourage people. I've been told on multiple occasions that my speech or presentation was inspirational, that it touched people's hearts and that it was funny at the same time. I love doing that and I feel comfortable doing that.

I used to be very shy and nervous, but, nowadays, I'm a confident speaker.

"Motivating and inspiring people, and making people laugh is what I would really love doing, if not as a speaker, than maybe in a different way, maybe as an entertainer, comedian, or singer."

Isn't motivation what people need most? Let me rather call it "uplifting". Maybe you want to start this with sharing your life story with them?

"That, sharing my life story, is what I am doing through this book. It's a good start, but I think I can do more.

"I have even secretly thought that maybe I could become a female priest in our church, if they'd allow females to be a priest. I would love to take the Bible and explain the meaning in clear and understandable words and in a way that relates to our lives now. I would do this by taking stories out of the Bible to inspire people to lead a better and more fulfilling life, instead of taking the Bible and make it all about a God who may or may not exist. I would like to make it more practical and understandable and put it in modern wording.

"The current priest in our church is absolutely brilliant in explaining things, and I have a lot of respect and love for him. I also admire him for his dedication. But there are still certain words that are not really clear or that are so old fashioned that they have lost meaning for me. I would like to talk in clear, modern language so that everyone can easily understand."

I see you smiling.

"Haha, yes, I'm smiling because it would be a great thing to do, and I believe that more people would be interested in reading a Bible that's explained in easy-to-understand language.

"So, yes, becoming a motivational speaker—in or outside of church—is something that has certainly been on my mind for some time. I also know that that isn't something I could become overnight, and, to be honest, I wouldn't even know where to start.

"Then, I've also strongly felt that I'm going to write two more books. I already have the titles in my head, and I would love to write these books to help other people live a more fulfilling live."

What would this book, your first one, be about?

"The book would probably be about living from the heart."

Give me more details why you'd write this book. Would you write it to just make you satisfied and happy? Or is there something more in it for all those reading it?

"The book would be about motivating people to live more from the heart and to dare being more authentic. And yes, of course, it would make me feel satisfied and happy as well. I would feel like I had contributed something valuable to the world, to improve the well-being of others. So, yes, I won't deny that my ego would love that as well."

Now, you have spoken about your working life here in Australia. What were you doing back in The Netherlands?

"When I left school, I got a job as a receptionist/secretary. It was a job for a small organization and I had a fairly good time. The company was some sort of test station for different grass types, corn, and some other things. It was all pretty informal. On sunny days, I could come in shorts and put my desk and phone outside. And twice a year we would all go out on the field to sow new grasses. That was always a lot of fun. We would all work together from director to cleaner. On those days, we would typically start early at 2am in the morning, and then going home early in the afternoon. The colleagues were really nice. I think the only negative was that I didn't have a lot of self-confidence, and I was always afraid that I would make mistakes. But, as such, it was a great place to start my working life.

"Then in 1986 I got a job in my hometown where I grew up. I had a job as assistant-manager HR. The job itself was great; there was a lot of variety and it was never boring. However, my manager was a real pain. He would have me do the same work multiple times and, every time, changed his mind on how it needed to be done. I know he didn't like me, and I certainly didn't like him.

"I learned a lot during this job. It was here that my interest in IT was sparked. In HR, we were meant to create a lot of different reports. We had the IT department setup reports using data stored on the MS-DOS computer. At that time, however, most data was still kept on paper. I quickly understood how IT created the reports and I started creating my own. I also talked to IT about having more data stored on the computer and how to do that. The IT guy was really surprised that I understood all of that and that I was able to create my own reports without their help. He suggested that I should pursue a career in IT.

"I also became the company's first aid officer. This wasn't something just on paper. I really had to put my knowledge into practice. People would come to my office with issues ranging from a simple paper cut to cut-off fingers and people falling of ladders. One thing I learned about my self was that, no matter what happened, I was always able to keep calm and give that first aid.

'During this job, I started studying Business Information Systems. I guess my interest in IT had been sparked, although I was also very interested in psychology.

"From there, I got a job at a software house as business analyst and quality manager. I worked for this organization for almost ten years, until I came to Australia."

Tell me about the other thing that you did. During the weekends, you also worked with children who had learning difficulties. How did that happen?

"It wasn't something I planned to do. One thing just led to another thing. My sister asked me if I was interested to joining her on the first Touch for Health / Kinesiology course, and spend the weekend together while, at the same time, learning something new.

"I said yes. It's always great to spend some time with her and the course sounded very interesting. At the time, she wanted to attend the course because she felt that it might benefit her son who was born premature.

"We had a great time, and I was hooked. We enrolled for another course on the spot, and from there on I think I attended about nine or ten different courses.

"When my younger daughter went to primary school and turned out to be dyslectic, I started using the techniques on her that I learned from Kinesiology. The results were pretty amazing, and completely changed her ability to read and write. Later in life, she learned another language and did advanced English for her HSC in high school. She also has a university degree.

"I practiced as much as I could. Then I ended up on Saturdays working with kids with learning difficulties. But my certifications had no value here in Australia. To get certified here would have cost me in excess of $35,000 and would have taken four years of study. Unfortunately, at that time, I just didn't have that money."

Reflection:

- **Life doesn't need to be perfect to still be valuable.**
- **It's in imperfection where the biggest lessons can be learned.**
- **Don't judge a book by its cover.**

Shaken Up

***

You certainly had a few ups and downs in your working life as well.

Now, please tell me about the coaching business. I know you'd like to avoid talking about it, but as I've said before, not willing to talk about it means you haven't really processed it yet.

"I know, and I'll talk about it. It doesn't hurt anymore, and I have long ago forgiven my business partner. I'm just hesitant because I don't want it to come back and bite me…I don't want him to come back and bite me… or kill me…"

Kill?

"Yes, kill me…Although it may not seem logical, it's a real threat that I'm taking seriously. I'd rather be safe than sorry.

"Like I said before, after I finished my coaching training, I started first doing presentations at gyms, which provided me with a few personal coaching clients.

"Then I also organized a booth at an event with other coaches. At the first event, there were only two coaches besides myself At the next event I organized a booth and 16 other coaches joined me to co-share the booth and costs.

"I had long talks with one of the other coaches, and, at the end of the event, he asked me if I would be interested in working with him to build our business together. I decided that it couldn't hurt to explore the idea, especially because he was more focused on business coaching and I was more focused on personal coaching. He also had been coaching for a longer time, so I could sure learn a thing or two from him."

And you did learn from him, didn't you? At the time, you didn't even realize it, but now you're very aware that you learned a lot from him. I know that you've taken a lot of these learning onboard.

"Yes, I did learn about coaching and generating new ideas and being creative. However, the best thing I learned from him was being more assertive. Well, I didn't really learn that from him. It was more a by-product of working with him, and having to deal with him.

"In the beginning, all was going well. We created business cards and other marketing materials. We developed a website and we also developed more coaching materials. And I started writing a business book. We were meant to write that together, but as he was working more on the website and marketing materials, I concentrated on the book.

"My business partner was the creative one, and I was the more organized and structured person in our business. He was so creative that he would come up with new ideas about every hour….yes, every hour. But he also liked to change his mind all the time. In the end, that didn't work for me. We didn't really get anything done because he changed his mind all the time. We had lengthy discussions about that, and, more and more, these discussions turned out to become very heated.

"More and more I had to put my foot down because his ideas were often unrealistic. I was also very concerned because we didn't get any new clients. Funny enough he wanted to have everything in order before getting clients, like the website and all materials. I, on the other hand, thought that this could be done in tandem with getting new clients and actually start coaching clients. I had done that before and that had worked well. You don't need to have a perfect business set up before providing services. In the end, a business can only survive when you have clients, start selling, and make money.

"Then, one night, we were meeting in the city after a network event to discuss yet another new idea. We had a bite to eat and I remember him getting us drinks. I had a glass of red wine.

"At one point, I had to go to the bathroom, I remember zipping up my pants and then all went black. I don't remember what happened after that, but when I woke up, I was in my bed. Very strange... I knew I didn't have too much to drink. I only had one glass of red wine.

"Then I unpacked my bag and discovered a paper. This paper stated that I acknowledged that I hadn't contributed anything to the business and that all business materials including the book in progress would be handed over and from now on would only be owned by my business partner. It stated that the business was dissolved and that I would hand all rights to him. At the bottom, I found my signature, his signature, and the signature of a witness.

"I didn't remember anything. I didn't remember what had happened that night, I didn't remember coming home, and I certainly didn't remember signing that piece of paper.

"When I called him, he stated that I had been fully awake and aware when I signed. He actually told me that it had all been my idea. He also said that after I signed I decided to go back home.

"Up to today, I still don't know what really happened. To be honest I really do think that he drugged me and forced me to sign. Why would I sign a paper like that? It certainly wasn't in my best interest."

That was really confusing and scary as well. But tell me, that wasn't the end of the story was it?

"No, it wasn't. Strange things had happened before, like he knew things about me that he really couldn't know, things that I had never told him."

But there was something even before that. There was a distinct moment when his attitude and willingness to work with you changed. Tell me about that.

"One night, I think it was after a network meeting, we decided to have a meal and a drink. He really had too much to drink and was no longer in control. He even said that he loved me. But he was so drunk that I doubt any of that was true. I had to take him back to his home in a taxi. He wasn't happy at all and became very agitated and upset. He told me repeatedly that he didn't like losing control and that I shouldn't take him home. It was really strange. I'd never seen anyone losing control like that. The only thing I wanted was to ensure he would get back home safely.

"Anyway, from that time on, we were fighting about almost everything and it all went downwards. He didn't agree about anything I would say and he would criticize everything I was contributing.

"Like I said, strange things started to happen. He knew things about me and my daughters that I was sure I never told him. For example, I had to buy a new microwave because the old one had broken down. Then, when I was talking to him over the phone, he asked me why I had bought a new microwave, as I didn't have much money. The thing was that I never told him I bought a new one. And there were other times he said things, indicating he knew things I never told him. In the beginning, I didn't think too much of it, but these things were starting to happen more and more frequently, and they became noticeable."

And then it got worse...

"Yes, it got a lot worse. After I lost my part of the business, we were threatened. My daughters got harassed by men on the street whom they didn't know. One guy sat with one of my daughters at her bus stop and told her that he knew her and that he knew what shampoo she used in the shower. He told her to tell me that I could never go to the police about the coaching business. If I'd go there anyway, all three of us girls would be very sorry and be killed.

"I had a good friend do a background check on my ex-business partner, and when he came back, the news wasn't good. My ex-business partner was likely to be an ex-agent of a foreign government. It was also very likely that he had put listening devices in our apartment. As I didn't know what to look for, I had my friend go through my apartment and look for it. And yes, he surely found them.

"As for going to the police, I thought long and hard about it and decided against it. I didn't have good experiences with the police who hadn't taken any previous phone threats seriously.

"As I knew my ex-business partner was always easily getting bored, I decided to do nothing at all, and not even call him or react in any way. That seemed to work, as after a couple of months, the threats stopped."

You also got advice from someone else, who told you that the best thing to do would be to do nothing at all.

"I contacted a psychic woman whom I had talked to before years ago. I contacted her because the two times I talked to her before, she had told me things that I had never told anyone before. The first time I met her, she told me about the vision I had about the planet of Love. She talked about it in so much detail, up to the colors and the feeling, the bubbly golden love coming out of the bellies and the new being that was created. I was absolutely stunned about what she knew about it.

"The second time, I thought I was just having a fun reading. That happened around the time when my boyfriend was starting to act strange, and I was starting to suspect that he may be gay or bi-sexual. The psychic told me that a male figure in my life was exploring his femininity and that there was a good chance that he would prefer men over women.

"This time I contacted her, because I hoped that she could give me some insight in my business partner and about what best to do. The first thing that she said, before I could even ask any question, was that I had to be very careful with a certain man in my life. She felt that he could be a colleague or that we could be working together, and that he couldn't be trusted and, more so, that he was a very dangerous man. She told me that my life could be in danger if I would act aggressively toward him. She told me that the best thing I could do was nothing at all.

"Again, she was so spot on with her description of him, that I believed her. This is also because that was exactly what I was feeling."

Are you sure your business partner didn't know her?

"Yes, I'm pretty sure about that. I never told anyone about it. There also was no physical proof in the sense of a business card, brochure, or anything like that. So I don't believe that he knew about her."

"I did just that; I kept quiet. I didn't contact him; I just acted as if nothing had happened. The harassments stopped after a while, and, as such, our lives went back to normal."

That was a very scary time. You acted in the right way. Doing nothing was the best thing you could have done. By now, you have also been told that he may be a member of the Mafia. Agent or Mafia member...it doesn't matter. He is someone you have to be wary about. So, well done for listening to your instinct! You didn't really have any real proof, but you listened to your gut feeling. I know how difficult it still is for you to trust these feelings.

What impact did this have on you and your daughters and does it still play a role in your daily life?

"At first, it didn't look like it had any impact at all. After being scared for the first couple of months, things settled down. We kept quiet, and we didn't hear anything from him again. And, after a while, we no longer got harassed.

"I think it was only after a couple of years that the effects became clear to me. My older daughter always double locks her doors and where possible she also has locks on her windows. We all have locks on our doors, but then I noticed that she also keeps her doors locked during daytime. I'm not saying that this is the only reason, but I believe that, for her, always locking her house up may very well have been caused by the ordeal we went through.

"My younger daughter told me that one day she came home from work and was no longer able to find her pajamas that she had left on her bed. She absolutely freaked out and actually called me up in tears. Fortunately, it turned out that her husband had put her pajamas in the washing machine.

"As for myself, I thought for a very long time that it hadn't really impacted me, until one day. I came home from work and found the gate of our property closed, while we never close the gates, and the dog beds were moved as well. For a moment, my heartbeat went up, and then I realized that if anyone wanted to harm me, they would most certainly not close the gate and move the dog beds. In this case, my husband's ex-wife came by to pick something up, and she had the habit of closing the gate. She also moved the dog beds.

"In the end, I think it certainly affected us all in different ways. I'm probably the one who coped best with the situation. It breaks my heart that my daughters have been affected negatively. It's a painful thought.

Reflection:

- **We learn most from the hardest situations.**
- **Trust your gut feeling.**

All I Got Is Love

***

There's one person you haven't talked about too much just yet. I'm talking about your husband. He has been and still is a major positive influence in your life. Please tell me about him.

"That's true. It's amazing how the love and support of one single person can totally change your life.

"I met him online. I had been on a dating site for several months and had met a few men that way. Unfortunately, no one really interested me. I felt no spark or emotional or intellectual connection. I know that this may not always come at a first date, so with some men, I went out on a couple of dates. But no one seemed to be suitable.

"One day, I just had enough of it and decided to delete my profile from the dating site. At that very moment while being online on the site to delete my profile, I received a message from my now husband.

"We had a couple of email conversations and I was impressed and interested to meet him. His English was perfect, even though he is German. He had lived in several countries and I could tell immediately that he was an intelligent person, and, from the way he wrote, he appeared to be structured, logical, and very warm and kind. That really appealed to me.

"So, we decided to meet. We went to the beach that first time when we met, and we had a great time. It really clicked for me from the first moment. I felt like I could really talk to him about everything and anything. He also had a pretty dry sense of humor that matches my sense of humor just perfectly."

So, how did you proceed?

"Over the next one and a half years, we grew closer and closer and I started to trust him. That certainly took a while, as it was hard for me to trust anyone at all. So, the fact that I couldn't trust him at first didn't say anything about him but, instead, said everything about me.

"Then I moved in with him. He offered that because my older daughter had moved back into my place, and with all her stuff and my younger daughter also still being at home, the space was all a bit too small. There wasn't too much space at my place.

"My boyfriend, at the time, was commuting between cities and would only be home every third weekend. So, I basically had his place to myself. I loved it. It was quiet and peaceful, and I think the environment had a positive effect on me.

"About 5 months later I moved in for real. My daughters had both also moved in with their boyfriends, and there was no longer any need to keep my old place.

"Then, after 5 years of being together, he asked me to marry him, and then a few months later we tied the knot. We had the most beautiful week with twenty of our closest family and friends. It was absolutely amazing. The weather was great, everyone was getting on really well, and we had the best time. It was a time I often think of. I know that some people talk about a fairytale wedding. Well, that was exactly what I had. It was all perfect and harmonious, and I still get this very warm feeling when I think about it. But, most of all, I'm so immensely honored to be his wife..."

I know. He truly is the love of your life.

"Yes, he is. It's amazing how two people can live together in such harmony. We've never had a fight in all the years that we've known each other.

"He is the most beautiful man. No matter what happens, he's always there for me. He helps me, stimulates me, and makes me a better person. This is really a major thing for me. I've never felt that protected or cared for in my entire life. I know that if something is going on with me, if I need help, that he'll always be there. I just hope he understands that I'll also always be there for him.

"We're each other's best friends, husband and wife, and, at one point, we were even colleagues. It's so absolutely wonderful to be in this warm, loving, supporting relationship. It's better than anything I had experienced ever before and anything I thought could ever be possible."

Why do you think that is? Are you alike or the opposite of each other? Tell me how you see this.

"We're very much alike, and share the same values. That's very important. We also share the same type of humor. I love how he has the same wicked sense of humor as I have. We often have a lot of fun together about things that other people may not even notice. I remember one day, when we went to the local hardware store. There was a sign outside that said, 'Every Saturday, DIY Adult Workshops.' As soon as I saw it, I looked at my husband with a big smile on my face. He was laughing as well. He immediately understood why I was smiling. See, a lot of people wouldn't understand why we thought it was hilarious. Other people may even think that our fun was distasteful.

"The point is that I never have to explain why I think something is funny. He's just thinking the same way as I do, so no explanation is required. That, by the way, also happens with negative things. When there's something I don't agree with, or think is bad, then one look at his face makes me realize that he feels the same way."

That means you don't even have to talk to each other. And that you might not even be able to hide because he knows you and your thoughts.

"That's true. But I don't want to hide from him because I want him to love me for who I truly am. I want us to have an open and loving relationship; therefore, I have to be open enough for him to know me. I have to trust that he'll love me, even when he sees things that aren't that pretty. That's not always easy, but I really want to continue to have and to work on an open relationship.

"We both enjoy traveling. I love to go on a trip with him and explore new places together. Traveling makes me feel free. We both traveled quite a bit before we met, but we've now also been to many new places and countries together.

"He also is pretty stubborn. That may be an issue for some people, but not for me. I recognize it because I'm pretty stubborn as well. When either of us is stubborn about something, the other one often makes a joke out of it, which lightens the situation. The thing is that I really understand it. I don't necessarily agree always, but I understand where he's coming from. I guess he also understands that from me.

"I've learned so many things from him."

What's the most important thing you would say that you've learned from him?

"I've learned to trust again. That's a really big thing. About 6 months into our relationship, he asked me if I trusted him, and I had to say no. I explained to him that that didn't mean he wasn't trustworthy. It was just that I had a lot of negative experiences in my life with other people, men and women, and that it would take time for me to totally trust him.

"Right now, we're more than 7 years into our relationship and I can truthfully say that I trust him. I know that he also made mistakes and will make mistakes, but I really believe that he'll be the best person he can possibly be, and that he'll also be truthful. That means a lot to me. It has changed me. Not only has our relationship grown, but I've also started to trust other people again. His example has certainly contributed in me having fewer issues trusting others.

"He showed me, when I had lost faith in humanity earlier in my life, that there are good people around. I got to know two great friends of his. They've been there for my husband in the past, and I know that they're both real friends who will help when they can. It's great knowing them and seeing a friendship that's so honest.

"I also got to meet the members of the church my husband attends.

When we met, it was too early for me to come along to church services. I also didn't quite understand why he was going, until he explained that the Bible is a guideline for life, and shows how to be a better person. He explained that it isn't about God telling us what to do or not to do. It slowly started to make sense to me. He also always spoke with so much love and compassion about the church community, the members.

"After about 2 years of dating, I was eager to come and see what it was all about. Today, I'm happy that I did. I'm also so grateful to have met the members of the church. Attending service and meeting everyone has truly restored my faith in humanity even further."

If I hear this right, he never asked you to come with him, but you decided to do so. Is that correct, and was that important to you? Also, I haven't heard too much from you about your relationship with a church. How do you feel about this?

"Correct, I decided that I was ready and open-minded enough to go to church with my husband. It was important to me because I wanted to understand better why this was important to him. And, now, it has become another thing that we have in common.

"I have a lot of love in my heart for every single person. They're kind, warm, and accepting. And I'm very thankful for who they are. Meeting them has had a huge positive impact on my life. I feel that I'm finally around likeminded people. And another positive thing is that whenever I attend a service, I learn a bit more about life and about being a better person.

"I also know that I can talk to the priest about any problem I have in my life. I still find this hard to do, but who knows what will happen in the future.

"Another thing I really like about my husband is that he's smart. He has a lot of knowledge and it's nice to talk to someone at a level that goes beyond beer and football. He's very logical and rational as well. As I'm also pretty logical, rational, and analytical, it means that, at an intellectual level, we're very compatible. We have great conversations, which I truly enjoy."

So you can and will just do what he suggests?

"Haha, no, not exactly. I can come to him with any problem I'm facing, and, when I have to make a decision and I'm not sure, I can always count on him to talk it through with me. He's smart and kind and loving, so I trust his advice. That doesn't always mean that I follow his advice. If, in the end, it doesn't make sense to me, I'll follow my own opinion. However, I always appreciate his advice, as it gives me another, sometimes better, insight.

"Last but not least, I totally love how he's always willing to help other people. So often, he's helped out my daughters and their families, whether by helping them move, doing little jobs in and around the house, or giving them advice. He's always there for them too. The same is true for his friends; he'll always try to help them as best as he can.

"I'm so grateful I met him. He's a good person. He's loving, caring, kind, funny, smart, and I love him with all my heart."

Reflection:

- Be grateful for the good people in your life.
- Real love will change your life for the better.

My Body Is A Temple

***

We've talked about a lot of things already, but you haven't really talked too much about your health just yet. What's going on there?

"I believe I was a healthy baby, although I was very tall – 56 cm - and skinny – 3 kg. From memory, I was a healthy little child up to the age of 6. At the age of 6, I was sick multiple times, and I clearly remember that. I had the measles and issues with my eyes. I'd often have a cold, and I ended up in hospital twice, once when my tonsils were taken out and the other time when I had an issue with my intestines. I also had one leg longer than the other and my spine wasn't straight, for which I had to wear a brace when I was a teenager.

"Up to the age of sixteen, I was probably fairly healthy, but then I started to have really bad colds and sinus infections. The doctor would give me antibiotic treatments, until one day, another doctor told me that that wasn't too good, and said it would be better just to use steam and some eucalyptus oil to clear my airways. Pretty much every year, I'd also get the flu. It was like every bug around would affect me. Having a fever always caused me to pass out. I remember one day when I had the flu and a fever, I was walking down the stairs at home and passed out. Thankfully, I didn't really fall too far.

"Looking back, I think I burned out. I burned out because of all the pressure my mother put on me to be perfect. I could no longer live up to that. I remember feeling miserable in every single way; I was shy, felt insecure, was sick all the time, and I felt that I was no good and too stupid to do anything good enough to live up to my mother's standards.

"Then probably around the age of thirty, I stopped getting the flu. I had one really big one just before and then it stopped for years. The next time I got the flue was when I had just arrived in Australia. They say that when you move to another country, you can expect to get sick. Apparently, the new environment can make you sick, until your body adjusts. But that was a really bad flu. I was sick for almost 4 weeks and had very high fever.

"Then after this time until now, more than eighteen years later, I never had the flu again. Yes, I have a cold now and then, but never the flu."

What happened over those years that you believe stopped you from being sick all the time?

"I think as a teenager, me being sick all the time was caused by stress. Later on in life, I really started taking action to keep my stress levels down. I was reading a lot of self-help books, and was working on myself and my well-being. I gained in self-confidence and I became a lot stronger mentally. I believe that all contributed to being more physically healthy as well."

So, you're linking mental and physical heath. But mental health isn't only about how we feel. It starts earlier with how we want to feel. What I'm saying is that we can condition ourselves to some degree to be happy or not and, thus, sick or not. Do you see this as well?

"Absolutely, I do see that. By now, there's no doubt that the mental state impacts the physical state and vice versa. And other than that, the way we want to feel also creates a condition. When we're unhappy but imagine what it is to be happy and imagine this over and over again, then we condition our being to be happy again. Obviously, this works the other way around as well. That's why it's so important to control our thoughts and, particularly, our negative thoughts.

"I've said before that in my life, I've faked confidence until, one day, I was confident. I've also faked happiness until, one day, I was happy.

"My parents had this tile at home with a quote that said; "a happy smile opens all hearts". One day I decided to smile even though I didn't feel happy, but then after a while I noticed that it wasn't a fake smile anymore. I was smiling because I was happy.

"Another health issue that I had when I was in my early thirties was food allergies. I was allergic to almost everything I ate and went on a very limited diet for many months. Today, I think I'm free of food allergies and can eat most things. I cannot eat shellfish and have to be careful not to eat too much citrus fruits. In particular, I cannot eat oranges. Other than that, I no longer seem to have any food allergies."

That would be great. Did you have this checked again?

"No, I haven't checked this yet. I need to find a place where they do an allergy test that checks the reaction in your blood over a period of 48 hours. This is important because, sometimes, the allergic reaction or intolerance doesn't show immediately.

"From the time I was around sixteen years old of age I was also always tired. Since I was always sick at that age, I didn't think much of it. It was only later that I realized that it wasn't normal at all to always be this tired. I remember that, at times, I wasn't able to go and visit friends or to go swimming with them. I was just too tired. All my energy had to go into schoolwork. Yes, I did go and visit my friends, but it wasn't as much as I would have liked to, and any physical activities were only making me feel more exhausted than I already was.

"Later on, I blamed my fatigue on my busy lifestyle with two little kids, a husband at home, a full-time job, and full-time university."

But you never thought there was anything you could or should change?

"At that time, I just had to get through university. My life would be less busy after that. I had hardly any time to think. I was just going and going on. Anyway, what could I have changed, drop out of university?

"Over the years there were other small to bigger health issues, like gallstones, an issue with my uterus, twisted ankles, and so, but nothing major."

But?

"The only bigger thing was that I had to have a full shoulder reconstruction. I must have been around 32 years old when I started having severe pain in my both my shoulders. It almost felt like they went out of the sockets and then flipped back in. I never got it checked out at the time, as I no longer had any faith in doctors. This was, by the way, also the time I started to get more and more tired. Even more tired than I had been before."

But you did nothing about it?

"By that time, I had lost faith in doctors, so you're right; I didn't do anything about it. I was just in a bit of pain that wasn't even constant pain. I also still had complete movement, so I never thought it was broken.

"It was only at least eighteen years later, when I was about 50 years old, I started to have real problems with my shoulder. It presented itself as severe headaches and pain in my neck. When I visited my general practitioner for my headaches, I was sent to get an MRI of my head done. This didn't reveal anything at all. But this time, I had a doctor who didn't leave it at that. As I was also complaining about shoulder pain, she sent me for a scan and an ultrasound of my shoulder.

"At that same time, I also started having issues lifting my right arm. When driving my car, I would have to lift my right arm and hand up to the steering wheel with my left hand. I was unable to do that with my right arm itself. Thinking back, it was really crazy that I was still driving. It could have been very dangerous."

So, finally something changed with regards to your ignorance of physical issues?

"Hahaha, okay, yes, you can say so, but only because I had severe issues moving my arm. The scan and ultrasound revealed that I had a tear in my shoulder muscle, so the general practitioner wrote a referral to a shoulder specialist. A visit to that shoulder specialist revealed that I didn't only have a tear in my shoulder muscle, but that same muscle also was no longer attached to the bone. On top of that, the specialist said that, at some point, long ago, my shoulder had been broken. According to him, the tear in the muscle was caused by the bone splinters that slowly but surely had started to slice the muscle in two."

Okay, stop here. You had pain in your shoulder but didn't get it checked until at least 18 years later?

"Uh, yes."

Why didn't you go and get it checked out?

"The reason was that I had no time, energy, or money, and I didn't have any faith left in doctors or specialists. Also, the pain wasn't continuously. It was kind of coming and going. Sometimes there wouldn't be any pain for weeks or months, until it would flare up again.

"It was obvious that I needed surgery. The surgery itself went fine, but there was quite a bit of pain afterwards. I put on music and also listened to binaural beats to ease the pain. This at least helped a bit.

After 6 weeks in a sling, I could finally start to have some physiotherapy. The exercises where pretty good and about 6 months after the surgery, I had full function back in the shoulder. Only after I had regained full function of the shoulder, did I realize how restricted my movement had become over all these years."

You compromised your health, as you've been doing repeatedly. You're still compromising your health.

"Yes, you're right."

Wow! You're saying I'm right? That's new.

"No, that isn't new at all. I often believe you're right. And as you're the part of me that knows, you're probably always right. Miss Smarty Pants!"

"But in my own defense, I often didn't take care of myself enough because there were other people depending on me, like my daughters.

They would always come first. Also, in my defense, I'm starting to learn to take better care of myself. This is a lot easier now that there's more time and money.

"It's a steep learning curve, though. But I honestly do take more action to get medical help or mental help. I meditate, and I've even taken time off to take care of myself, have some rest, lose weight, and get fit again."

And...?

"And, what?"

What you put in, you get out.

"Food you mean?"

Yes, I mean food, that stuff you eat.

"I try to eat as healthy as possible. But my relationship with food is a difficult one. First, and no excuses here, I love nice food. I particularly love my cookies, cakes, and cream. I have this re-occurring dream, or nightmare I should say, where I enter a large room with tables full of delicious cakes, and I'm allowed to eat as many as I want to. I'm so happy. I see all those cakes and I'm not restricted, but instead can eat whatever I like. But then my mother enters the room and tells me that I can only eat one cake. I always wake up so disappointed.

"However, I'm not the person to go for fast food; I'll have McDonald's maybe twice a year, and a pizza maybe five times a year. I never really used to eat a lot, and, for a very long time, even after the birth of my children, I was more on the skinny side. I even got comments from colleagues that maybe I should eat a bit more.

"That all changed after I went hungry. I guess that my relationship to food had changed. Food became a tool for survival. From that time on, I would have a very hard time putting any leftovers into the bin. I'd rather eat them than throw them away. As there then was enough or even too much food later on in life, I started eating way too much.

"I know what I'm doing. I'm very aware, but it isn't easy for me to throw food out. So, I'm trying to buy and prepare only what I really need. But that's hard as well. I tend to buy too much because, today, there's money to do so. I'm still working on an approach to have a healthier relationship with food.

"The other issue that keeps me from eating healthier is my fatigue. Because I was working full time and spending a lot of time traveling to and from work, I hardly ever cooked. I was just too exhausted. The only thing I really wanted to do when I got back home after a day's work was to go to bed and sleep. As I still needed to eat, I often had a piece of bread at night. I knew that it wasn't the best thing for me to eat. It provides me with too many carbohydrates.

"I've now started to order healthy food that I hardly need to prepare. Hopefully that will help me to lose weight in the long term."

Does this all work for you? I remember us eating things we shouldn't.

"It's still a learning curve to get it right, but now I'm losing weight and I hope to have better control over my eating patterns. I also try to eat as healthy as possible. I'm not following any specific diet anymore. I felt that all of these diets limit me in one way or another. Instead, I eat in moderation a wide variety of foods to get a variety of vitamins, proteins, and carbs. At this moment that seems to work.

"I've also started to go out for daily walks. The aim is to get fitter again, lose weight, and work on my strength and flexibility."

What about your teeth?

"What about my teeth?"

You know exactly what I mean.

"Yes, I know. My teeth are a concern. I haven't really been to the dentist in about 18 years. Well, that isn't entirely true. I did go about 4 years ago. My husband kind of tricked me into it. He knows that I'm extremely scared of going to a dentist. So when he had an appointment, he told me to meet him at his dentist, which was on the way to a restaurant where we would have dinner after his appointment.

"I didn't suspect anything, but he had made an appointment for me as well. I wasn't mad at him, because I understood his good intentions. Nonetheless, I absolutely hated it. I agreed on just having a check-up, so that the dentist could see if any work needed to be done. As expected, my teeth were certainly not in a good condition, and it was expected to cost around AUD 25,000 to repair it. I reluctantly agreed to have my teeth on the lower right side all fixed, as this seemed to be the side that required the most urgent attention."

Did you feel happy with your decision?

"The decision was double. Happy is certainly not the right word to express how I felt. Scared is probably the better word. I am happy though that it is all done, and at least a part of my teeth are okay now.

"You have to know that that was a really big step for me, and I only agreed to it if intravenous anesthetics where administered. The procedure happened just a week later, and that went reasonably well. I don't remember much of it. What I do remember vividly was when I had to come back to get my crowns put on. I totally panicked and had a real panic attack. They gave me gas, and only then, I very reluctantly agreed to get the crowns put on.

"After that, I never went back. I know that there still is a lot of work to be done, but I really don't want to go, unless they totally knock me out and fix everything in one go."

I know you're unreasonably and terribly scared of the dentist. Do you understand why this is?

"Back in the Netherlands at the time I was a child, I wouldn't get any pain relief for fillings or any other work that needed to be done. So, it was a very unpleasant experience. Also, I'd always be in pain for a long time after the appointment. They said I couldn't be in pain anymore, but I always was.

But I guess if there's one thing that could have really triggered it, then it was the appointment that I had when I was 6 years old.

"On the inside of my upper lip, my skin of the lip had grown onto my gum. The dentist needed to burn that away. I remember lying on the chair, and he told me to open my mouth. I saw him standing there with that little torch in his hand. I saw the flame and refused to open my mouth. Then he started shouting at me, and a nurse came to hold me still. He said that if I didn't open my mouth myself, he would have to force me to open it. My mother was just standing there, not trying to help me. I felt betrayed, yelled at, and abused. As you can imagine, it was painful and it smelled... yes, like burned flesh."

It's obvious that you have some issues here. What are you going to do about it?

"I'm not sure yet. Some dentists specialize in dealing with people with extreme fear, so if I really, really have to go, I'd only go to one of those specialized dentists."

You just told me that you do need to go. Why do you now say "if"?

"Alright, *when* is probably the right word. I just don't want to think about it. If I have an option to go under general anesthetics, I'd have no problem. But that doesn't seem to be an option. And then things like meditation to calm me down and hypnotherapy to take away my fear may help.

"To be honest, I'll probably only look at these things when I really have to."

Let's come back to that. You said you have to go, and it's overdue. Delaying will not change anything other than keeping you in this fear for longer than necessary. You can't avoid some things in life and need to face them.

"I know you're right, but it's easier said than done. It's certainly not something I'm ready to address right now. I understand that isn't the smartest approach, but that's all I'm willing to do right now."

I hear you, and although I also don't believe that's the smartest move, I understand, and I'll leave the subject for now. Tell me about your mental state.

"Obviously, life hasn't always been easy, and I've sought help from hypnotherapists and psychologists in the past. I especially needed help after my daughters moved out of the house and moved in with their boyfriends. I also moved out of my place to move in with my boyfriend. So, this was meant to be a very happy time, wasn't it? But no, I started feeling very depressed.

"I guess that because I no longer had the primary care of my daughters anymore, I felt reasonably useless. It was as if my life were over. My daughters had long been the drive to go on, to be strong and courageous. I was all they had, and I had to take care of them. Now that that responsibility had substantially decreased, I didn't know my role anymore. Who was I? What did I want to do with my life? I needed to find a reason to live my life for me, instead of being alive to take care of my daughters.

"That was very hard at first. I had never really taken care of myself. This was something I had to learn. I also had to learn that I deserved to take care of myself. I had to find new goals, hobbies, and things that I liked. There had never been any time or money for that, so I really had to discover what I liked and what made me happy. I had to learn to love myself."

You're still learning and discovering, but you're getting better and better at it. And, you've certainly found reasons to keep on living. Yes, I know that suicide has been on your mind more than once. I also know that you would never really commit suicide because you would never do that to the people you love.

Back to you being so tired, can you tell me a bit more about it?

"Like I said, it probably started when I was about sixteen, or maybe even earlier. I also remember being extremely tired after the birth of my younger daughter.

"The thing is that I can never tell when I'm going to be too tired to do anything, when I'm going to be so tired that I really have to lay down. Sometimes, I'm already extremely tired when I wake up; other times, the extreme fatigue only starts later during the day. Extreme fatigue means I cannot function anymore. At those times, I don't just feel tired, but I also have a very weird feeling in my head. "Sometimes, I even can't drive home without taking a nap first. These are the extreme times. But I'm tired at all times. I never feel rested; I never feel energetic. Thus, everything I'm doing seems to be a struggle. I'm forcing myself every day to get up, go to work, and try to live my life as normal as possible.

"Now, I've taken an extended break from work to try to get more energy. Unfortunately, after having been home for more than two months, I still don't feel any better. I still get extremely tired for no apparent reason, and it still seems to happen at random times."

Tell me about your sleep. You know that your disrupted sleep patterns also play a role in your fatigue.

"You're right. I don't sleep well and that, of course, has an effect on my energy levels. I truly don't understand why I'm still not sleeping well enough. I do fall asleep within five minutes, but then I wake up about two hours later and I have trouble falling asleep again. I do fall asleep after that, but wake up about six to eight times a night, after which I have trouble falling asleep again.

"Four years ago, I visited a sleep specialist, who discovered that I stop breathing 58 times an hour and that I wake up 33 times a night. I got a CPAP machine to help me with my breathing, and it really improved my sleep. So now, I only wake up six to eight times a night. That's a big improvement, but I clearly still don't sleep well enough. The specialist told me that the CPAP machine would solve all problems, but there certainly is something else going on here as well."

This machine helps your breathing. That's a mechanical function we need to live. It doesn't make you sleep, it only helps you doing so. Sleeping is a time where our mind needs to rest as well. Maybe you can even say that your mind need to sleep before your body can. What do you think?

"Well, both the mind and the body need to rest. However, the mind may not rest when the body rests. When you're dreaming, your mind is in full swing. But I do agree that the mind needs to be calm enough for your body to be able to fall asleep.

"There are times, I'm stressed and can't stop thinking, but other times, I'm really relaxed, but just can't get back to sleep. Sometimes, it's so bad that I only get two hours of sleep, and other times, I'm up for most of the night. But even on those days when I don't have a small nap during the day, I often still don't sleep well the next night. You'd think I'd be exhausted, and I am, but I'm still not able to have a decent and, more importantly, refreshing sleep."

Exhausted doesn't mean tired. The latter makes you sleep, the former makes you unhappy.

"I'm not sure if I understand the difference. Can you please explain?"

What I mean is that to be truly "just tired" makes us sleepy. Exhausted is much more of a mental state, one in which we're stressed but not really tired. The mind of someone exhausted is still in full swing. But, as you say, we need to have a calm mind to fall asleep. To fall asleep, we need to be tired in mind and body. Awake or exhausted isn't the state to be in when you want to sleep.

"I also take melatonin, do breathing exercises, and mediate. Still, nothing seems to really help. It's an ongoing issue that I haven't been able to solve. Solving this may well be the key to solving my fatigue. In spite of this, I still go on with life the best I can. I still go to work, do the groceries, and just live a fairly normal life. However, I know I'm pushing myself every single day. Yes, every single day!

"Will writing about my life, writing about my stressful events help me to deal with anything I haven't truly dealt with, including my fatigue? I guess there's only one thing I can do to find out, and that's finish this book and truly and honestly document everything that has happened in my life, or at least the most painful, important, as well as the beautiful and loving moments.

"What I do know is that I won't give up until I really understand it and until I have enough energy to live the life I want to live. I may not have all the answer right now, but a part of me is confident that I'll be able to get answers and solve this fatigue once and for all. I'm currently taking action in a less conventional way. These experiences will certainly be part of my second book."

Reflection:

- You get out what you put in; rubbish in, rubbish out.
- Taking care of your health means that you take care of every aspect of your being.

Leisure For My Pleasure

***

We talked about a lot of different things, mainly about all the events in your life and how you feel about the people around you.

There are a lot of things that you've done, but tell me a bit more about what you really like to do, about your hobbies.

"You want me to tell you about what I really like to do? Okay, let me think about that.

"This is a hard one because there never really was time to think about what I really like, and about what I really like doing. My life, for a very long time, was consumed with simply surviving. Time, for me, was a very rare thing in the past. Now I have more time on my hands, but a lot of that time is still spent working. And yes, I know that normally one would have time left after work, but I'm normally so tired that the only thing I feel like doing is watching TV.

"I think that I'm also still discovering what I really like doing. On top of that, there are many things that I'm interested in trying. That doesn't mean that I'll really like them.

"I have a very broad interest, and also like to do things I've never done before. I like a little bit of a challenge by doing things that I have no knowledge off and then try to get that knowledge in a short time. I might fail, find out that I'm not good at it, or that I don't like it, but I enjoy trying out a whole range of different things.

"Lately though, I feel that working with mainly my head no longer satisfies me. I'd love to work more with people and with my heart. But now I'm not sure what that could be. What I am sure of is that working with people is something I truly want to do.

"Other than that, I love to sing and dance. Traveling and other cultures and languages also are my passions. I always feel the need to explore and discover, and I can never have enough of that. Retirement is slowly coming and I'm really looking forward to that. We'll have more time together, more time for traveling and doing the things that we enjoy. I'm not sure, though, if either of us would stop working entirely. We may not work fulltime anymore, but I'm pretty sure that we would find something else to do."

That's interesting now. You told me all the things you'd like to do with your life. Are you aligned there with your husband? Do you know what he would like to do?

"We're certainly aligned here. One of the main things is that we're ready to take it easier and not work that hard anymore, and, most importantly, spend more time together. It's pretty clear that, for both of us, the most valuable thing is to be together and enjoy each other's company.

"We've talked about our retirement many times, and I think we're both getting ready. We both love to travel, and I know that he'd like to join a choir with me so that we can both sing. It doesn't mean that we've totally planned out our retirement. As I said, we may decide to do some part-time work still or to volunteer. I can't see us sitting at home and doing nothing.

"Other than spending time with my husband, I also love talking to people and hearing their stories. I find it often intriguing to hear what other people have to say and find out what they're about and what they've done in their lives.

"Modern and Eastern medicine and meditation are also things I'm really interested in. Unfortunately, I haven't had time to really understand or do more with it. In that line, I also love to coach and inspire other people.

"From a creative point of view, I love to write and create small websites. Not that I'm really good at creating websites, but I do enjoy the creative process.

"More intellectually, I enjoy logical puzzles and Excel spreadsheets, and, most of the time, I'm interested in learning something entirely new."

I don't think anybody else would mention Excel spreadsheets when talking about hobbies. But then, there aren't too many couples like the two of us, right?

"Hahaha, so now we're a couple too? Funny enough, both my husband and I love Excel spreadsheets, calculations, and creating scenarios. For example, I have a spreadsheet with my weight and weight loss best and worse scenarios calculated and put in a chart. I know I'm not the only one doing these things, but some people would probably think it's strange that I enjoy doing these things. My husband keeps track of his finances in Excel spreadsheets, and I used to keep track of my budget. So yes, it may seem like a strange hobby, but I enjoy doing all types of calculations in Excel.

"When it comes to nature, I love both the sea and mountains. Unfortunately, I live too far from the sea. That's a pity because the sea always makes me feel calm inside. The sound and the smell really relax me.

"I also love dogs and cats and all types of other animals and plants and flowers."

You sure have broad interests, but there must be things that you really aren't interested in. Can you tell me about those types of things?

"Of course, there are also things I'm not really interested in. I'm certainly not a technical person and, in general, I'm not too interested in really technical stuff. However, my husband loves technical things like engineering, cars, electricity, and the like, and he talks about it a lot. So, even though not intentionally, I still learn a lot from him.

"Other than that, there isn't really anything I wouldn't want to know more about. On the contrary, I'm interested in learning and discovering so many things, that it's always hard to decide what to focus on next. So, in general, I guess you can say I have a pretty diverse interest."

Reflection:

- For couples it is important to have common interests. The older you get and the less you have to care about children, the more important this becomes. If not, a couple lives parallel lives, become complete couch potatoes, or split.

I Belief In Miracles

***

Another touchy subject is "Belief."

"Well, when you say belief, I don't think that's too much of a touchy subject. However, when you're talking about religion, then that's a different matter."

Yes, I know what your opinion of religion is. The question is whether or not this opinion is correct.

"Okay, I hear what you're saying, and, in principle, you're correct, but an opinion isn't necessarily correct. It's a viewpoint or viewpoints of a single person or a group of people, and it doesn't necessarily reflect the truth.

"I'm not pretending I know the 'truth.' My opinion is merely the truth as I know it, formed by the information that I possess."

So, what's your "truth"?

"There are several aspects to what I believe in. To start with, I think a lot of people confuse belief with religion, as I've mentioned before. I believe (think) that there's no ONE belief because every person is different and, therefore, everyone will believe different things. For example, I can believe that the train trip from A to B was enjoyable, while someone else can have a completely different experience and believes that the train trip was annoying.

"Religion, to me, is an organized institution with a set of beliefs that's common or very similar for a certain group of people, and has to do with the belief in a higher purpose and/or a godly type of character.

"To be honest, I don't really want to talk about religion. I think there are too many fights and wars fought in the name of religion. Let me tell you what I believe instead....

"First, I believe that there are many questions about life and the universe that go unanswered, and I often feel that when one question is answered, it then may bring up a whole set of new questions.

"Second, even though I'm not a fan of religion as such, I do believe that we should all try to be the best person we can possibly be. And, as such, I agree with many things that have been written in religious books.

"Third, I believe that that are many things that we as humans aren't aware of, cannot see, don't hear, and maybe are unable to even comprehend."

Okay, not bad. Let me give you a reaction to each of your three statements.

First, you're wrong! You already have all the answers to any and all question you may have. Your belief that you don't have all the answers lies in the fact that you don't completely comprehend who you really are. You have a limited belief of who you are.

Second, yes, you're right; we should all aim to become better, more loving persons. However, this is strongly linked to the desire of spiritual human beings to experience, grow, and evolve. Every new day is a new chance to grow and become a better person.

Third, you're partly correct. In order for you to grow spiritually and to experience, you cannot know all there is to know. I know that this may seem like a contradiction to the first point where I say that you already have all the answers to your questions. What I meant by that is that you can look up answers by accessing your 'library.' However, you wouldn't give a child who's just starting to read, a highly technical book with lots of difficult words. In other words, you can only experience and learn what you're ready to experience and learn. However, you're able to experience many more things than you believe you can experience. I'm talking about the things you believe you cannot hear, see, or comprehend. Even though the child cannot read nor understand the highly technical book, it can start reading other books at the appropriate level and then progress to read books that are more 'difficult.' Of course, these books then are no longer difficult, as the child learns more and more and advances level after level. In other words, you could enhance your level of awareness by taking it step by step.

"Okay, yes, the way you explain it makes sense to me."

Good. Now, let me ask you another question. Do you believe in God?

"Hmmm, I was waiting for this question to come up. First, I want to say that I was raised in the Dutch Reformed Church, so as a Christian, I learned about the Bible and about God and Jesus. I was kind of taught to believe in God.

"However, I had many questions and there were many things that really didn't make any sense at all to me. For a long time, I didn't want to go to church or have anything to do with God, because it truly didn't make sense to me. If God really exists and is so powerful, then why is there so much suffering?

"Is there really a God who created the universe? If so, where did this God come from? How was this God created? Logically this didn't make any sense to me."

And your husband has answers for all this, since he attends services?

"No, my husband doesn't have any answers either. No one has. No one knows for sure if there's a God, and if this God created the universe.

"And when it comes to religion, why do we need to be baptized, why are there rituals like the communions in the Catholic Church? Why do we need all these ceremonies proclaiming in public that we believe in a God? Is it so that we can be part of a group? That really doesn't make any sense at all to me. These are rituals that don't have any meaning to me. I understand that these rituals are symbolic. But being part of that doesn't mean you're a good person. I have seen many people going to church on a Sunday or Saturday, who were not nice at all. For me, if I wanted to believe in a God, I could do that without all these rituals.

"What I also strongly disagree with is that in some religions, women are still discriminated against. Often, women still can't fulfil any roles in the church such as priest, elder, or the like.

"The church I currently attend also discriminates against women. Women for example cannot have any official function within the church, and during sealings, a woman has to wear a cloth on her head while a man doesn't need to do that. Although I love going there to learn how to be a better person and to connect with the other church members, whom I really love, I would never truly become a member, as long as women haven't been given the same rights. I find it a real insult and disrespectful, and, as a church, they should know better."

You husband has a different opinion on that, doesn't he?

"Yes, he believes that you can only change things when you become part of it. So he believes that I should be become a member of the church to be able to change their attitude toward women from within the church.

"I hear him. I understand what he's saying, but, unfortunately, joining as a member so totally goes against what I believe in that I'm unable to see beyond that obstacle...at least for now.

"And although I follow some of their rules within reason, I won't follow rules that I find disrespectful or totally uncomfortable. For example, I'll never wear a hat or stockings like other women in this church do. I will, however, wear a dress, as I sometimes also wear a dress outside of church hours. But if there comes a time when I find it too uncomfortable or too cold to wear a dress, I certainly won't hesitate to wear pants.

"What I do believe in is that going to church will remind me of being a good person or a better person. And there are many life lessons to learn from the Bible whether you're religious or not, whether you believe in a God or not."

Let's come back to my question if you believe in God…

"When I think about the questions I always had about the creation of the universe and of the world as we know it, the creation of life, I have to admit that I don't know how it was created.

"Logically, it would need to have come from somewhere at some point in time. But you can't have nothing, and then, suddenly, there's something. You can't have no universe and then, suddenly, out of nowhere, there's a universe. You can't have no God and, suddenly, there's a God.

"What I'm saying is that I don't have one single answer to any question about the creation of life. I don't know how life came to be. If I don't know this, then I also don't know how and if God was created or always was, or if there even is a God at all.

"I actually should have as many reasons to believe in God as I should have not to believe in God. In other words, I cannot logically explain the existence of Life, yet there's life, and I cannot logically explain the existence or non-existence of God, so there may be a God."

Does it actually matter if there is a God in whatever form and shape? What would be the impact on your life – every day and every moment?

"I'm not sure if it would have any impact at all. To me, it is better to not believe in a God and try to be the best person possible, than to believe in a God but live a selfish life. What I'm saying is that the existence or nonexistence of a God shouldn't impact who you are as a person.

"I have as much reason to believe in a God as I have to not believe in a God. I simply don't know. For that matter, I have to admit that there may be a God, a higher being, who may or may not have a physical form.

"To be honest, I think that if there's a God at all, then this is probably more like an energy, a source. Or maybe God is a synonym for all there is or the force that connects us all. I don't see God as a being on a throne. The way I understand it now is that God is Love, God is all there is, God is the highest vibration.

"I realize that the above may be a bit hard to understand, but the main message here is that I now believe that there could be a God, as much as I believe that that isn't possible."

Yes, I understand; you're a very logical person and you've always had a problem believing that there could be a God. For you, belief has always been more about being a good person, learning from your mistakes, being kind and loving, and sometimes sacrificing your own well-being for the well-being of others.

Now, another question; do you believe in Jesus, Buddha, Muhammad, and the like?

"I certainly believe that these people existed once in time. I see them more as spiritual teachers than as religious people, even though we think of them as religious masters. I believe that they are still known and stand out till today because their wisdom and kindness was far ahead of their time. Many people now could certainly learn from them. I can still learn from them.

"For example, for Jesus to preach love, kindness, and forgiveness in the barbaric times he was living in must have been really hard. But he showed us the way of a more loving life. He also showed us to stand up for our beliefs. In that respect, he was and still is a real teacher today. Standing up for your own beliefs, even if this goes against the commonly accepted beliefs or values was, and still is, not an easy thing to do.

"Buddha and Muhammad had the same type of wisdom to share, and every single person can still today learn valuable lessons from them.

"What came out of their minds and their hearts became a guideline for a purposeful, harmonious, loving life. And even today, we can learn from them to become better persons ourselves."

Now tell me, you pray as well, don't you? Can you explain why you pray and why you believe praying is a great thing to do even if you don't necessarily believe in a God? To me, it seems almost that you're saying one thing, but then you're doing another thing. What I'm saying is that you really aren't convinced that there's a God at all, but, at the same time, you're praying, and I know that in your visions and meditations you have conversations with Jesus. How does that all fit?

"I understand that, to a lot of people, this doesn't make any sense. But you of all, as you know everything there is to know, should be able to understand it. At the moment, it looks more like you're accusing me of being dishonest by saying one thing and doing another thing, which you think is a contradiction of the first."

No, no, you got it wrong. I'm not accusing you of anything; I'm merely stating a fact that may seem like a contradiction. I'm just asking you to explain it so that other people can understand.

"Alright then. First, I'd like to state that I don't know if there's a God, as I explained before. So why do I pray? Well, I have also explained before that I believe there's more than we can see, hear, or even feel. I explained that I believe we live multiple times and that life and the universe is so complicated, that no one actually really understands it.

"I've also talked about how I speak to the universe, which I believe is the same as praying. When I was younger I never believed praying would be useful or would have any affect at all, but later on in life, I noticed that when I pray, something does seem to happen. I have experienced that repeatedly.

"Are my prayers answered by a God? Maybe. Are my prayers answered by loved ones who've passed over, by angels, or by certain energies? Maybe. The fact is that I don't know who answers my prayers and gives me the help I need.

"But guess what? Praying does help! Praying is like asking for help from God knows whom. Praying has helped me in several situations. A great example was when I prayed for help when I didn't have work lined up, and a taxi driver helped me. Another example was when I needed surgery and was scared."

Maybe you want to pray before going to the dentist. (smile)

"Hahaha, you have me cracking up here. You are cheeky!

"At first, I always asked for exactly what I wanted, but I've come to believe that there's a better way of praying, which I'll share with you in just a moment.

"I've said before that I believe we don't always consciously know what's best for us, so instead of praying for a specific outcome, I now pray for the best possible outcome. This idea didn't come from me though. I just don't remember where I read this. So unfortunately, I cannot acknowledge this person. But it seems to work for me, and, therefore, I'd like to share it. It goes something like in this example below:

"Dear Universe,
(Or instead of Universe, you could say God, Angel, Source, or anyone or anything that can help)
Can I please ask for the most benevolent outcome for my health?"
(You can replace health with family, job situation, finances, anxiety, anger, wellbeing, relationship with_____, etc.)
"I imagine that the most benevolent outcome will make me feel happy and healthy and pain free."
(You can replace happy, healthy and pain free with wealthy, worthy, loved, relaxed, excited, appreciated, etc.)
Thank you.

'For me, praying in this format has given me the greatest results. I have to warn you though. You don't always get what you expect. The answer to your prayers may come in a completely different form.

"For example if you pray to get a specific job, you may not end up getting it. You may be disappointed, but trust that there's something better on the horizon at some point, even if that isn't directly right now.

"If you're used to praying, you may have found better or more effective ways, but the type of prayer I shared with you here seems to work for me. Many times in the past, I've been able to solve problems, forgive people, and get a good outcome using this format."

Reflection:

- Belief isn't the same as religion.
- Love is the biggest force.
- God is Love, God is all there is, God is the highest vibration.
- We need to strive to become better persons every single day.
- Every new day is a new chance, a new beginning.
- Nothing ever stays the same.
- Pray for the most benevolent outcome.

Wisdom Beyond Age

***

Can you please share with us your biggest life lessons?

"Two of my biggest life lessons I learned from both my daughters. One big lesson I learned from my younger daughter when she was about 15 years old. I have to admit, at that young age, she was a much wiser person than I was with my 42 years of life experience.

"At that time I was struggling with a big decision, and I couldn't really make up my mind. Someone I had recently met asked for my help. I had known this person for only about two months, and the request came as a bit of a surprise.

"He had to go to Africa for work, and shortly after he had left, I received a call from him from a hospital. He had been robbed and mugged. His passport, wallet, and mobile phone were stolen, and he suffered major head injuries and broken ribs.

"I don't remember his full story anymore, but apparently, he no longer had access to money or to his bank account, but needed to pay hospital and surgery bills. He asked me if he could borrow $4,000, which he would pay back as soon as he was back in Australia.

"Although I didn't have any savings, I could take that money out of my credit card. $4000 may not seem like a large amount, but, for me, at the time, it was huge. I had only just found a reasonable paid job and was still paying off debts. But as this person seemed genuine and obviously sounded under a lot of stress, I decided to help and transfer the money.

"Two weeks later, however, I received another distressed call. He not only required additional surgery but also had contracted malaria. So, he made another request for financial help. This time, he asked for $8,000. That meant I would have to stretch my credit card to the limit, and get a cash advance that would accrue a high interest rate.

"Then I tried to call the hospital to ask them to email me the invoice. They hadn't heard of him... I called all hospitals in the city where he stayed. No results. That's when the doubts started to appear. The hospital didn't know his name? That's strange! Was he really in a hospital? Was his name really his name? Or did the hospital make a mistake and did he genuinely need help?

"When he called again, I confronted him with my suspicion. He then told me that they had misspelled his name, but that he had received the invoice himself and that he would email it to me.

"He emailed the invoice to me and, yes, his name was misspelled. Or maybe not. The quality of the invoice was very bad, and it almost looked like the name on the invoice was changed. I couldn't tell for sure though.

"In the meantime, I hadn't transferred the $8000 he asked for, as I was torn. Was this person a scammer, or someone very unfortunate who desperately needed help? I didn't know anymore. Thinking about it, I would change my mind about it every single minute: *he is a scammer; he needs help; he's taking you for a ride; he needs your support; you'll never see your money back; he's hurt and needs your money...*

"Many thoughts were running through my mind, but I couldn't make up my mind. Who was he? What was he: a scammer or someone who needed help? I didn't know. I didn't know what to do. I truly couldn't make up my mind.

"I remember sitting in my bedroom thinking about what I should do. Then, my daughter came in and saw that something was bothering me. When she asked, I explained to her the situation and the decision I had to make: to transfer money or not.

"She thought for a moment, and then she said: 'I know the answer; I know what you'll do.' I was surprised. How could she know what I would do?

"She said, 'It's very simple.' She took my hand and put me in front of the mirror. She asked, 'who do you see, Mom?' I said, 'Me of course.' 'Exactly,' she answered, 'all this time, you've been asking yourself the wrong question. You're asking yourself, "Who's this person," but you should be asking yourself, "Who am I?"'

"I didn't understand. 'What do you mean?' I asked. She said, 'If you really don't know who this person is, you can fall back on knowing yourself. Are you a person who can live with losing money or are you a person who can live with the thought of having let someone down who potentially really needed your help? To me, that's no question, because I know who you are, and I know what decision you'll make.'

"Some people may say that it was stupid to give him that much money, and that I must have been totally out of my mind, but, in the end, my daughter was right. If you don't know how to react in a certain situation, if you don't know what decision to make, the best thing you can do is to be true to yourself and to your belief of who you truly are. That was a great lesson.

"Another great lesson was one I learned from my older daughter. When she was about 15 years old, she came to me and told me that she wanted to see a counselor. I said that she could talk to me instead, but she said she preferred talking to someone else. So, I gave her a list of counselors that weren't too far away and made sure I provided her with some information about these counselors so that she could see which one appealed most to her. We than made an appointment and I would drive her there.

"The lesson here was twofold: First, if you need help, you need to ask for it and/or take steps to receive help. People cannot read your mind. Second, if you're providing help it doesn't always have to come in the form of you personally helping. It can come in the form of directing that person to a better source of help. In the end, the well-being of that person is the most important.

"In this case I was very happy that my daughter asked for help and that she trusted me enough to ask for someone else to provide her with the help she needed."

I remember these moments, and I remember that you were awed with admiration for your daughters, who shared wisdom well beyond their age.

Reflection:

- Know yourself and be true to whom you believe you truly are.
- Ask for help when you need it.
- Help can also mean directing someone to a better source of help.

I Feel Good

***

In the end, where does it all come to? As your story is such a complex one with so many aspects, can I ask you a couple of questions to sum it all up, and give us your insights?

"Yes of course, go ahead. You know me, if I don't want to answer any of your questions, I simply won't. So no harm done to me."

Oh oh, here we go again…Do I now still need to explain to you that I would never want to harm you?

"No, of course not. I was just joking."

Okay, just making sure.

What would you say were your biggest challenges?

"The biggest challenges for me were to keep on believing in myself, even though everything seemed to be against me. Also, having to go to work and live my life while being so tired was pretty hard. This still is very hard. And, during extremely stressful times, it was often hard to take enough care of myself so that I wouldn't break down completely."

What things hurt you the most?

"The things that hurt me most were being hungry, the way my mother treated me, and feeling utterly lonely."

What things do you consider your biggest achievements, or what are you most proud of?

"I'm proud of doing full-time university studies while having two little kids and a disabled husband at home and having full-time work. I'm proud of getting back on my feet time and time again. I'm also happy that I was able to forgive my mother, and to open my heart to trust again."

What are your biggest regrets?

"I don't really have any regrets, other than for the times that I hurt other people. Even though life has been pretty hard at times, I have learned from these times and they have made me who I am today. So, no, I have no regrets. I've been blessed with a very interesting eventful life and I feel grateful for all the experiences and beautiful people in my life."

What would you do differently?

"In general, I would make more of an effort to take care of myself, my own well-being, and my health. I would try to be less stressed, especially about what other people may or may not think, and I would try to enjoy life more than I've done in the past."

What are the most beautiful moments of your life?

"The most beautiful moments of my life so far certainly are the births and the relationships with my daughters and grandkids, my relationship with my husband, the connection with my sister and her kids, and the vision I had of pure Love. I feel so blessed and grateful."

We've covered a lot of different things and you have tried to honestly talk about your life as you have experienced it. Are there any final words of wisdom you would like to share with your family and your readers?

"Yes, I would certainly like say a few more words...

"Whatever you're going through in your life, I would urge you to be true to yourself. I would like you to be the person you really are or want to be, instead of trying to only please other people.

"I would like you to be strong and courageous, do the things you really want to do even when others don't agree. When you feel that it's the right thing to do and it doesn't harm anyone else, then go for it and don't let anyone stop you.

"Love yourself for who you are and for what you do and accomplish. What may look like only a little thing to you may actually turn out to be something very big, if not to you than maybe to others.

"Be kind and loving toward others. This world needs kind and loving people. The biggest gift you can give to anyone, including yourself, is to love unconditionally.

"Try to be a better person every single day, and learn from your mistakes.

"Forgive other people for their shortcomings, and don't forget to forgive yourself when you're at fault.

"Never stop learning. Learning doesn't only bring knowledge; it also brings joy and pleasure. It means that you're evolving.

"Be accepting toward others and other opinions. They may be as right as you are.

"Enjoy the little things in life: a cup of coffee, a child playing, music, the smell of a flower. If you can find multiple little things you can enjoy during the day, you'll be a happier person.

"Never, ever, ever give up!

"Try to live life in the here and now, and give it your all.

"Don't forget to have fun, and don't forget to laugh out loud and often.

"And finally, don't fear the end, as you have only just begun…

***

"As we come to the conclusion of this book, I'd also like to express my gratitude to what you have done for me, how you have helped me, encouraged me, and gave me some tough love as well.

"I think that I have not only come to express and understand the events of my past, but I have learned a lot about myself, and how I can be myself more and more, and live a more fulfilling and loving life. I've also come to understand things from a different perspective, which has given me a more complete understanding.

"I'm grateful for every event that occurred, as they have formed the me I am today. I am also very grateful for all the people who crossed my path. Everyone in their unique way has made a contribution to my life.

"And last but not least I want to say thank you for your love and guidance. I love you."

I love you too. And never forget…

"Yes, I'll never forget that we are one, that I'm loved always, never alone, and that I can always ask for and receive help."

Thanks to us and the All that is.

***

Epilogue – Letter For Toé

***

Dear Toé,

When you read my letter to you, you may start to understand that I am you in a different here and now. Don't ask me why, but I truly believe that this book, my memoir, will reach you at some stage in your life. At the time of reading this, you'll understand that you are me in a different experience.

I've always been a believer—or must I say "knower"—that we all exist multiple times. Most people would talk about different lives, but I wonder if it would be possible to exist in multiple expressions of one soul at one given time.

The Bible says something like we can create what we can imagine. If truly so, you can say that I believe it's true that we can exist in many timelines and in many dimensions, even in multiple expressions of the same soul.

Let's assume for a moment that, in principle, I'm right, and all of that is possible, and I've never had any reservations that that couldn't be possible, then, my question has always been, "If my assumptions are correct, it should be possible to communicate with the other expressions of myself."

Don't ask me how. I just don't know. But I would like to know.

Even if we don't exist at the same time, but in a sequence in time, I have always thought that somehow we should be able to communicate with ourselves. They say that everything is energy. If we were able to connect our energies, then we should be able to communicate.

I believe that the dead can communicate with the living, I also believe that we live multiple lives. That to me implies that we could potentially communicate with ourselves if we were able to make some type of energetic connection between the life now, our state of "death," and our new next life or other life.

I was and am still intrigued by that idea. What if we could really communicate with the multiple expressions of ourselves? We could learn from our other's mistakes, we could share information and ideas and even communicate experiences. That idea totally blows my mind.

Am I crazy to believe that this all may be possible?

I had a vision of you Toé, the me in a "future" lifetime. And if you ever find this writing, I'd like you to know that I love you and that I respect you. What you do is absolutely amazing.

You're a spaceship navigator, a very good one, but more than that, you're known in the far corners of the universe as "The Negotiator." You negotiate for peace between the different species, and you're very successful and respected amongst many of these different species.

You're also hated, because not all species want peace. Your life is in constant danger, and you never know from what corner the danger comes.

To counteract that and for your own sanity, you practice some type of meditation. I've seen your quarters on the spaceship, and it's a space of quiet, soft, and calm strength. I see how you meditate on a mat in this soft-lit room.

You're a half-human, half-alien man. Your girlfriend looks human, but has more alien DNA than you do. I know, I know...you don't use the word *alien* anymore. In your time, it's an insult. You have named all species.

It's strange to realize that, for you, in your here and now, alien species are part of your everyday life. In my timeline, humans would freak out meeting an alien. Many humans will even doubt that there are any other intelligent life forms in the universe. There are movies about aliens, and, most of the time, they're portrayed as dangerous, trying to eliminate the human race. I guess, as with everything, there are the good and the bad. You'll know that and experience that on a daily basis.

Now that you're reading this, I also wonder if what I write makes any sense at all. Some of the questions about the universe I have and my experiences of things that are not touchable and often are thought to be unbelievable, in your world, may be common and accepted. I'm not saying that no one in my world would understand what I'm experiencing and that no one has the same type of experiences, but either they're rare, or people in general don't talk about it. I hope for you that they're no longer strange.

I also hope that you may find something in this book. Something that you can relate to, something that makes you smile, something that makes you realize and understand that I'm you and you're me, and we're one and the same soul, expressed in another experience. I hope that the words in this book will make you cry and laugh, and that, at times, you'll say, "Yes, that's me!" I hope it makes you understand that you're more than you can see, more than you can feel, and more than you can experience in just the one expression of yourself called Toé. I also hope that these words will contribute to you having a more complete understanding of yourself.

Who knows? Maybe one day we'll be able to truly communicate with the other expressions of ourselves. That would call for a celebration!

For now, I wish you well. You're in my thoughts, in my heart, and in my prayers.

Much Love,

Maxima

Afterword From My Husband

***

To my dearest wife and you, the reader of this book,

When my wife told me she is writing a book about her life, I was very curious. Once it came to a conclusion, she asked me if I wanted to read it and I obviously said yes. Well, it is very different for several reasons – as a reader you will see yourself.

I started reading and crying at the same time. What openness, what courage! It's easy to say or write "I am great". But what takes courage is to not only say how you really feel and what you love, but to admit fault, weakness, and how to get hurt.

In this book my wife has done exactly this, to a point where I could exploit this knowledge and hurt her. I feel immensely privileged as I know she only shared this book because she trusts me. And this trust gives her a strength most people don't ever experience. I saw her changing once the book was done – finishing the book and sharing her truth liberated her and gave her, I think, an immense sense of achievement.

And this is exactly my message to the readers of this book. Take the courage to be open and honest. You will not always win, but will always be the winner, simply because of your courage. Peace of mind cannot be bought or learned, it can only be achieved. Be brave, be bold, and be yourself.

Thank you Maxima, my True Love and Inspiration!

About The Author

Maxima Miller has overcome a lot of adversary, and has grown into a strong and happy person. She grew up in the Netherlands and now lives in Australia with her husband. She has two daughters and several beautiful grandkids. Maxima has a degree in Business Information Systems, and speaks multiple languages. She loves anything to do with self- and spiritual development, as she believes that there is always room for improvement and growth. If she didn't do what she's doing now, she would have wanted to be a brain surgeon as she has a keen interest in healing and medicine as well. Maxima is an author, coach, trainer, entrepreneur, designer and business analyst. In her spare time, she loves to spend time with her family, travel, read, write, and sing.

www.outofmyminds.com
www.spiritualsoda.com

Printed in the United States
By Bookmasters